THE BOSS' SON

REMEMBERING THE BOOTT MILLS IN LOWELL, MASSACHUSETTS 1937-1954

by
Roger Flather

authorHOUSE®

AuthorHouse™
1663 Liberty Drive
Bloomington, IN 47403
www.authorhouse.com
Phone: 1-800-839-8640

First published by AuthorHouse 6/28/2011

ISBN: 978-1-4259-6130-5 (hc)
ISBN: 978-1-4259-6131-2 (sc)

Printed in the United States of America

This book is printed on acid-free paper.

*Because of the dynamic nature of the Internet, any Web addresses or links contained in
this book may have changed since publication and may no longer be valid. The views
expressed in this work are solely those of the author and do not necessarily reflect the
views of the publisher, and the publisher hereby disclaims any responsibility for them.*

DEDICATION

TO:

My father, "the boss," and mother who married into the Boott
Mills saga

My four siblings and four Flather first cousins, who also lived
the Flather family management experience at home

My co-workers at the Boott Mills, who shared their lives and
work experiences with me

My wife Becky and four children, who have supported me
during my battle with cancer, enabling the completion of this
book

TABLE OF CONTENTS

ACKNOWLEDGMENTS

I am grateful to the Lowell National Historical Park, particularly to Carolyn Goldstein, Jack Herlihy, and Dan Walsh; to Martha Mayo, Director of the Center of Lowell History; to Jean Lambert of the Saints Memorial Medical Center which now includes the old St. Joseph's Hospital; to the family of the late "Incredible Mac," and to my four siblings and four Flather first cousins who graciously shared their memories and family perspectives.

I am grateful to a very large number of incredible staff at Memorial-Sloan Kettering Cancer Center who cared for me this last year while I battled cancer with a steady schedule of chemo treatments. I am particularly indebted to Dr. David Kelsen, my oncologist, Dr. David Kissane, my counselor, and Ms. Gloria Wasilewski, R.N., my ever attentive, outpatient nurse. Finishing this memoir became my cancer coping project that gave me motivation to pursue my life. These three professionals kept me on track.

INTRODUCTION

After my father died in 1979 and my mother started the process of moving to a smaller apartment, my four siblings and I proceeded to clear out the family home to make it ready for sale. In my father's attic office we found an old filing cabinet in which he had kept a file on each of his five children containing report cards, school programs, summer camp applications and other miscellaneous records from our childhoods. I removed my file and, without so much as looking at it, carted it back to New York City. For a long period of time, it remained unexamined.

Over the years, I had on numerous occasions told my children about my experiences at the Boott Mills, both as a young boy accompanying his father there and as a teenager employed by the company. Several years ago, at their encouragement, I finally began to write down my recollections. Then, just this last year, I accidentally rediscovered the aforementioned personal file that my father had kept on me. More than twenty years after taking possession of it, I looked at it for the first time! It was then that I found a second grade homework assignment in which I had been asked to answer the question, "What Does Your Father Do At Work?"

The document had the effect of thrusting me into the past, all the way back to the very evening I had completed the assignment. I recall sitting at the foot of my father's bed, trying to put into words what he did at work. As he read over his business papers before retiring for the night, he explained his job to me. For this reason, the paper spoke to me factually and emotionally as no other input from the past possibly could.

It was as if my father were here in person to communicate with me, telling me about the way it was, how he approached his work and what values he held foremost in importance. The recovered homework assignment has given my writing project greater credibility. It remains a treasure to me today and serves to inspire this book both intellectually and emotionally. It does not get any better than this. Thanks Dad.

I begin with my memory of being taken to the mill for the first time, when I was four years old. Over the next thirteen years there were numerous visits to the mill by my father's side. I walked the products floor and was on hand for eye-witness observation of floods, the Army-Navy "E" award ceremony for excellence in production during World War II, a debilitating post-war strike that lasted eight months, and the installation of an expensive, long-range, economic innovation in the form of a conveyor system that connected all the production processes in an efficient and cost-cutting manner.

Many children do not know what their fathers and mothers do at work and never have the opportunity to visit the work place and see their parents at work. I knew what Dad did, where he did it, how he did it and the importance and value he attached to each work component. I was a lucky child and a lucky young adult to have had this exposure to my father, his workplace and his career.

The next part of the book covers my four years as a mill worker, beginning in 1950, when I worked every summer and school vacation, until 1954, when I graduated from college and went into the Navy at age 21. The mill ceased production for good at this time.

During this four-year period, I witnessed and wrote about

the steady, inevitable decline of the mill as a viable entity. I observed fewer workers, less production and more floors filled with ready to operate yet silent machinery. Finally production ceased when the decision was made to buy finished cloth more cheaply from competitive southern mills, rather than manufacture it in Lowell and sell it as a Boott Mills product despite its origins.

As an adult with many years for retrospection and benefiting from some research I was able to conduct at the Boott Mills Museum at the Lowell Center for History, I explore some family dynamics and try to pull together certain conclusions about the operation of the mill as a family business and its final demise in 1954.

Each of these treatments draws from a management family perspective. The contribution that I can make to the literature of the New England cotton textile history is to document a personal, less often told story from this point of view.

PART I: THE EARLY YEARS (1930s)

1. First Visit.

I did not do it! I did not shut down the telephone system at the Boott Mills but I do remember being taken to the mill by my father on that fateful day, on what must have been a childcare assignment from my mother. Once there, while my father went into his office to do his work, I was left seated on a bench just across from the telephone switchboard operator. This was the waiting area.

I watched her carefully as she inserted the long cords into the telephone panel and pulled them out when the calls were completed. I recall many bright lights on the panel, maybe they were red and green, or white. After a while she left the area and I was left alone. I suppose it was during this time that the telephone system crashed throughout the entire mill and since I was the only one there, I was blamed for it. I must have been all of four years old, old enough to remember, I think, if I had really touched anything. It is my earliest memory of the mill. Some dozen or so years later when I started to work at the mill I was reminded by my father and Tom Kenny the Superintendent, of my "crime" many years before.

2. At My Father's Side.

My father always referred to the mill as "the mill," not a factory, not a plant, not a corporation or a company. Most of the textile mills in Lowell were called mills, and the official name of the Boott complex was the Boott Mills.

My father had placed textiles deep in his soul. He enjoyed the process of making cloth and talking about it. Whenever I bought a new suit of clothes or an overcoat, he would place a sleeve between his thumb and forefinger and rub the material back and forth, commenting all the while on what the material consisted of and its quality. He must have started this process at textile school as a young man, and it became a habit or a part of his behavior for a lifetime. In so many ways his "perfect fit" into cotton textile manufacturing manifested itself.

I found in a family file a college essay, an autobiography my father had written as a freshman at Harvard College in 1919, in which he wrote about "an occasional visit to my father's cotton mill, a rare privilege of which few of my playmates could boast. These visits aroused my interest greatly and I now look back upon them as the cause of my desire to be a businessman, and more especially a manufacturer." My father, in taking me to the mill, was repeating what my grandfather had done for him many years earlier. My father seemed highly motivated at

4

a young age and destined to work at the Boott Mills following college. He knew early on and specifically what his career goal was to be.

He also knew from the outset that he was joining a dying industry and that his chosen career would involve an uphill battle all the way to the end some thirty-one years later. This all turned out to be true.

I remember numerous trips to the mill with my father. Especially in the summer, when it got dark late, he would tell my mother he needed to go to the mill and that he'd "take Rog along." As long as I was to accompany him it seemed my mother would acquiesce. We would go to his office first, walking across the narrow footbridge to the second floor of a small office building, just over the canal at the end of the parking lot. This building was called the Counting House. Near the walkway was a wider vehicle bridge over the canal. All supplies entering the mill, all finished products and waste leaving the mill, and all employees entering and leaving the mill crossed this vehicle bridge. It was a marvelous sight to see hundreds of people on this bridge when the shifts changed. Only the front office personnel, management such as my family members, and official visitors used the office bridge. Today this office bridge is gone and the second floor entrance door is bricked in.

Once in his office, my father would sit me down and proceed to do whatever it was that drew him there. Then we'd take a walk. He loved to walk the production floors, which would be running near or at full capacity, it being in the middle of the second shift. He would lead me around, teaching me about textiles and showing me off, although he didn't say this in so many words.

We would go to the warehouse by the railroad siding off of French Street first. This building has long since been torn down. Here, several freight cars would be parked with doors open and bales of cotton in view. On workdays, a couple of men would be wheeling the heavy bales into the picking room on hand trucks and the textile production process would start here.

The wires that held the tightly packed bales would be cut with large wire cutters that looked like shears, and then large clumps of cotton the size of sofa cushions would be pulled from the bales and loaded into the picking machines. These machines seemed to have dueling knives inside which would flash into the hard-as-rock clumps of cotton to open them up, and start to crudely align the fibers. Then the cotton, looking like a heavy dirty white blanket, would be moved by manual labor to the next process.

The opening up/picking room could be a dangerous place to work because the men (no women) worked in close proximity to those huge opening-up machines, and one could get hurt quickly and lose a hand or an arm if care was not taken continuously. The room, as I recall, was unhealthy and too hot. Cotton lint drifted through the air like a snowstorm. While I think the men wore face masks, I am not sure. Their heads and clothes were covered with clumps of cotton, and they looked like snowmen. I remember the men sweating profusely whatever the temperature was outside, despite the open door to the freight cars.

Fires were also a big risk. I cannot say fires were frequent because I don't know, but they happened often enough that prevention and fighting them were priorities. Fire-fighting equipment-- extinguishers, hoses and buckets of water-- hung on conveniently placed big *Wall Street Journal* bolts. This equipment was everywhere, but more so in the picking room than in other production areas. The risk of fire was sufficiently great that the opening room was always located in a separate building or area, set apart from the rest of the mill. This was standard mill procedure. My father made sure every time we went there that I knew this. When my father and I would talk about our mill tours with my grandfather and were on the topic of the opening rooms, my grandfather would always say, "The opening room, you know, is always separate from the rest of the production areas, in a building set apart, because of the risk of fire."

My father told me that the opening-up machine knives would hit rocks carried north in the bales of cotton, causing sparks. All that lint and soft dry cotton fiber floating around made for perfect tinder. One spark was all that it took to start a fire. During one of our visits, there was a fire, and I was fascinated. We stood with our back's against a wall while everybody ran about fast and furious with buckets of water, and almost immediately the fire was out, but the area was awash with water. I wanted to stick around but my father pushed me on. I guess it was time to allow the men to get things in order in the usual way, without the boss and his son standing there taking it all in.

We would continue our walk through the production process building by building (nine of them), floor by floor (up to six in some buildings), room by room, sometimes the whole route, sometimes just a section, depending on how much time my father wanted to spend, maybe until my bedtime. Sometimes my father wanted to check on something specific in one location that had to be attended to, which he wanted to follow up on firsthand. Perhaps something had happened such as a breakdown or accident for which repairs were underway, but would not be finished until the next working day. On other occasions, my father's route seemed determined by his desire to visit with workers he knew personally and had a special relationship with. He always liked me to meet these special people. He was called Mr. Flather by just about everybody but there were exceptions. These exceptions, these special people, were workers who happily and comfortably called him by his first name, Rogers. They did so because he and they had started that way back in July, 1923 when my father began working in the mill, having just graduated from Harvard College.

He had worked in various parts of production, just as I was destined to do years later, while he attended the Lowell Textile School at night after work one or two evenings per week, one to two hours each night, depending on his course schedule. Residents of Lowell attended the textile school free of charge in those days, while nonresidents paid nominal fees for classes taken. In due course, the Lowell Textile School joined with the Lowell State Teachers College to become the University of Lowell.

My father completed a three-year course of study that consisted of cotton design, cotton finishing, and dobby and jacquard weaving. While called weaving, this latter course was actually a course in loom fixing. He graduated from the textile school in April, 1925 along with his brother, Frederick

Jr., my Uncle Frederick. Frederick Jr. had also been taking classes and also had graduated from Harvard College, and had begun working in the mill in 1923. My grandfather, Frederick Arthur Flather, was a member of the Board of Directors of the textile school at that time. My father and Uncle Frederick would be assistant bosses under my grandfather, but not at the beginning, when they were heirs apparent and bosses in training. Both my father and Uncle Frederick worked without pay for the first six months of their employment, to learn the ropes of textile manufacturing and to prevent any bad feelings with experienced workers. It gave management some breathing space for the two new managerial family members to settle in smoothly.

So my father planned his visits to the production areas to go out of his way to meet up with the special people he had worked with and who had taught him so many years earlier about the ways and techniques of making cotton cloth, and who called him Rogers. He and they seemed relaxed together, and the expected boss/employee distance seemed nonexistent, in deference to the close co-worker bond established at the outset of my father's textile career. Afterwards he would tell me what he knew about these workers and their families, how they contributed to the production process, and how valuable they were to the mill.

One of these special people was a lean, erect, alert man with more years than a regular retirement-aged person would have, who worked in the machine shop. The machine shop was located on the ground floor in one of the back buildings, and it performed an important and central function in the mill. In many respects it was the heart of the mill. Here machines were repaired and in some cases built from scratch. People who worked in the machine shop were highly skilled, better paid than production workers, and more powerful in the union than perhaps any other textile occupation category. Power and prestige could describe their situation, and when the mill closed, they possessed the skills requisite for easily and quickly finding another job.

This special person who worked in the machine shop was impeccably dressed, with spiffy clean overalls, denim shirt, and a denim watch cap like what a railroad engineer would wear. He sat in an office swivel chair on a raised platform that reminded me of a small bandstand. From this perch located in the center of the machine shop, he could observe everybody and every task being performed throughout the shop.

The shop had a full range of metal-cutting, drilling, punching, and sanding machines and a number of lathes. The older man was beyond the time when he actually worked at a bench station, but from time to time he would leave his perch and join a worker at the bench to help solve a problem or give advice. He rarely did any actual work. His impact was verbal, symbolic and educational.

My father always went up to him first when entering the machine shop to say hello and introduce me. My father had a great deal of respect for this worker and would comment that he was one of the finest machinists in the textile industry. He called my father Rogers, so he was one of the workers who had been on hand to help orient my father to the textile industry in 1923.

One time, after we had both left the machine shop, I said something like, "What does he do? It seems like he just sits there." My father was quite indignant and corrected me harshly. He told me it was good for morale, the smooth running of the shop, and the maintenance of serious and safe work habits to keep this man on for as long as he wished, at his regular pay, despite his being well over retirement age. He had to have been in his mid-seventies. Management was in full accord with paying him just to sit there and be the present example of a machinist extraordinaire, to help out when needed and to pass the time doing nothing when he wasn't needed. If my grandfather up in the front office could stay on indefinitely, so could this machinist down in the machine shop.

My father further explained that he was available to consult and solve problems less-experienced machinists could not handle, but most important and valuable to the Boott Mills was the man's work ethic and work record. He had spent his entire work life at the Boott Mills, and his record was impeccable: hard work, initiative, integrity and supreme skill. He was to my father "old school," and the Boott Mills would happily and productively keep him on hand and pay him his full pay for as long as he desired to go to work every day.

My Uncle Frederick, I believe, also had his special people that he related to very closely. One time when I was talking casually with Tom Kenny Jr., a departmental supervisor and son of plant superintendent Tom Kenny, Tom Jr. said that he had especially enjoyed working on a difficult engineering problem with Frederick.

The union was controlled by the men who worked on machinery in the machine shop along with men such as the loom fixers who worked in every weaving room. When the mill was on strike in 1947-48, these men could moonlight at any number of mechanical jobs such as fixing appliances and doing automotive work, or travel to distant mills in New England. When the mill closed in 1954, these men were able to transfer their mechanical skills and easily find other jobs.

The workers who worked in the production rooms where the cloth was actually made, like the spinners and weavers, had fewer transferable skills to fall back on and were subjected to a kind of structural unemployment when the mill closed. There were no jobs for ex-spinners and ex-weavers. It was especially difficult for women whose future work in so many cases was limited to childcare and taking in laundry.

The point of making cloth is to get all the fibers from the raw cotton pointing straight ahead in the same direction, in one long endless piece. The process is one of picking, carding, drawing, maybe carding and drawing again, combing, twisting, spinning, dressing, slashing, seizing, whatever, to produce warp yarn (thread) that runs lengthwise on a warp beam, and weft yarn (filling) that wound on a bobbin runs crosswise in a shuttle on a loom, the weaving process. After the cloth is made, it goes to a cloth room for inspection and measurement. Here women with a special hand device that contained a set of sharp razor blade-like scissors, cut off loose threads. They could also cut out imperfect or blemished sections of cloth. Finally the finishing process would be completed: wash, bleach, dye, singe, brush, cut, sew, package and ship. Large trucks would leave the mill yard full of finished product.

3. SAFETY FIRST.

I liked visiting the card rooms. These were the kind of machines my grandfather worked on for the Pettee Machine Works in Newton Upper Falls, Massachusetts, when he was a young plant superintendent in the 1890's, well before he took over the Boott Mills in 1905.

The huge rounded card machine had a roller drum inside around which was tightly wound wire with many little spikes or barbs on it. These spikes straightened out the fibers. Over the top of the spiked roller drum was a cover plate set with very close tolerance to the spiked wire. The cotton leaving looking like the thinnest of gauze and was then gathered into a cotton rope called sliver. The cards had a special sound. Each machine in the mill had its own special identifying sound. The cards made a ticky ticky sound.

The card room could be a dangerous place too. If a finger or a hand got too close to the opening where the spiked wire disappeared under the cover plate, it could be captured and drawn up and under the close tolerance cover plate, flattening it. It brings to mind a crocodile capturing a prey. In one accident I was told about, that plate was cracked by the worker's arm, having drawn the limb in and up to the armpit before the machine could be shut down. I wanted to work in the card room, but I was told, "too specialized," meaning too dangerous. As I traveled around the mill with my father he would tell me these stories and preach safety. When I worked in the mill as a teenager years later, supervisors would tell me the same stories and preach safety.

My father liked to tell me about the worker who lost a finger in a machine. Later, as the worker was describing and showing how the accident happened, "I was doing this and then..." wouldn't you know it! He lost another finger. Every time my father told me this story, it was as if it was for the first time; he did not seem to remember that he had told it to me many times before. He would tell this story again and again. He told it on our mill tours, he told it at home. My father had safety on the brain!

My father talked incessantly about tools and safety. "A man had a screwdriver in his hand, pointed up, and when he leaned over his work bench he poked his eye out." My father would then demonstrate how this could happen if one were careless, without a tool in his hand, of course. This story too was related more than once. My father was, generally speaking, a conservative and cautious man. He was concerned about health and safety matters at home and at work. I used to think he was too careful, too cautious, even fearful, and it bugged me no end, especially when I was in my adolescent rebellion years. Years later, on reflection, when it was too late to tell him, I knew he spoke with much wisdom.

Throughout the mill there were safety signs. Factories can be dangerous places, and these included textile mills. Some of the signs indicated the number of days elapsed since the last industry accident. These signs were especially prevalent during World War II when there was a heavy emphasis on speeded up production. The customer, the U.S. government, or more specifically the U.S. Navy and the U.S. Army, wanted maximum production in an accident-free environment and generated safety programs to make this point. Posters noted (preached) that industry accidents limited production and were detrimental to the war effort.

During World War II, expanded war production required expanded employment, so there were large numbers of new, less-experienced workers on hand and a large turnover in addition. This could only lead to a high accident rate if extra-special precautions were not practiced. The number of Boott employees grew from perhaps 1,200 to 2,500 during the early war years and remained there until the government cut back production orders at the time of victory in 1945. The mill ran three shifts (i.e., twenty-four hours of production five and a half days per week). In one year, to maintain the 2,500 worker count, the mill had to process 5,000 people. The unavoidable turnover was due to the many male workers leaving for military service and workers, male and female, leaving for higher-paying jobs elsewhere in the defense industry, such as at the new government-built Remington Arms plant in South Lowell (later to become the Raytheon Lowell plant for making Sparrow missiles for the U.S. Navy), or shipyards in Fall River and Boston, Massachusetts, and Bath, Maine.

There were also safety signs about the water. Toilets and sinks for hand washing used river water, which was unsafe to drink, but all right to clean up with. In the winter this water was icy cold, and indeed I remember looking out the windows to the river below and seeing clumps of ice floating by. Over the sinks were signs that said, "Do Not Drink This Water," or, "This Water is Unsafe for Drinking," in English, French (for the French Canadians), Portuguese, Greek, and Polish, the predominant languages spoken by the mill workers at that time. There were also workers from Ireland, Belgium, Italy, Turkey, Lithuania, Sweden, Russia, Germany, and several other nations, making it a diverse work force.

Separate pure water fountains were available throughout the mill for drinking purposes, but could be at the far end of a production room. My father never passed a water fountain without taking a drink. He felt it was important to drink enough water each day.

4. CONTINUING THE PRODUCTION PROCESS – SPINNING.

On our tours, we would continue through the production process, observing the blanket of cotton being reduced in steps to wrist size then finger size rope, then finally into thread: laps to sliver to roving to yarn. Like the squeegee rollers of an old washing machine, sets of drawing rollers, each set turning faster than the predecessor, stretched the cotton out, reducing its diameter. It would all end up in the spinning rooms, where large spinning frames containing hundreds of bobbins spun the thread necessary for the warp and the weft of the follow-on weaving process. Depending on the final product requirements, different machines using different settings could produce different threads for weaving different materials.

All of these distinctions would be explained to me, but most of the time I was preoccupied by watching hundreds of bobbins being filled or emptied of thread with metal rings moving up and down in unison for as far as I could see. I was mesmerized by the process and unable to listen attentively and absorb much of anything. Years later, when I was older, I would get the same explanations and tutoring, but I never worked in the spinning room or on spinning machinery. I never learned the technical subtleties of these midway cotton manufacturing processes. When the threads were ready, they were wound on the warp beams, hundreds of threads running lengthwise (warp threads), or on to bobbins to run crosswise (woof thread). Weaving on looms was next.

5. Weaving on Power Looms.

The loom is really a simple machine that remained fairly close to its original design for many years, although with hundreds of technological improvements that were invented, patented and installed over time. Looking at a loom in operation, it is easy to figure out how cloth is made. The moving parts perform logical tasks, and the machine is wide open to view. Today's newer state-of-the-art looms are somewhat different, with more moving parts enclosed and hidden. They also utilize much faster shuttle operations and even two shuttles that only go halfway across, but pass the thread from one to the other when meeting before returning back to the starting place. Shuttles, once a foot or so long, are now more analogous to bullets than the larger projectiles of yore. Indeed, the traditional shuttles could become dangerous if the looms were not adjusted right. My father, weavers, supervisors and fellow workers all told me about real accidents or close calls they witnessed, when a shuttle flew out of the shed and across the room at eye level, until stopped by hitting a far wall or breaking through the glass of a window. The sharp, metal-capped pointed end of the shuttle could do some mean damage to the head of a worker in its path.

One of the more interesting aspects of weaving was the

control mechanism used to make patterns or designs or lettering in the finished product. In a simple weave, half the number of threads of the warp were threaded through one harness and the other half through a second harness. Thus, when one harness was pulled upwards a space was left, the shed, for the crossing shuttle to pass through. Then the harnesses would be reversed, and what was up went down and vice versa, creating a new shed for the shuttle to pass back through. Hence the weave.

More complex weaves were accomplished using half a dozen or more harnesses all preset to move up and down in a repeating order of combinations. The top of the harness had a leather strap that wound over a pulley and down underneath the loom to wood levers, which were moved up and down by a turning shaft on which were mounted cam wheels. These cams were designed with a round bump or two that could be located at different places around the circumference so as to control which wood levers, and thus which harnesses above, were operated in various combinations to achieve various woven designs. The harnesses were kept taut by springs that held them down until the cam-wood-lever-pulley arrangement lifted them up for an instant. Part of the classic sound of the loom is the clatter of these harnesses going up and down. This may sound complicated, but once seen will be comprehended in a flash. Also, on a handloom one can see how the foot pedals operate the harnesses in a similar way to the cams and levers on a power loom.

More creative patterns and designs were woven on looms using dobby heads. A dobby head was a device hung on the top side of the loom frame through which a continuous string of small ruler sized slats connected to each other on each end with a space between, rotated in at the top of the dobby and out at the bottom. This circular string of slats looked like a miniature snow fence one can see in the country and could be seven or more feet long.

The slats had holes into which preset combinations of metal pegs were inserted all looking like cribbage boards. The pins operated small metal levers inside the dobby heads, manipulating the harnesses for more intricate patterns than could be achieved by the cam/lever system described above. I could watch a loom with a dobby head for hours. I could watch a loom with the cam wheel system for hours too. Years later when I worked on looms, I used to carry those cam wheels around for the loom fixer I worked with as a helper. The cams were heavy. After extensive use, the bumps on the cam wheels would get worn down requiring replacement, or perhaps the design in the cloth was changed which could also result in the need for bumps located in different places.

In the early days of my visits with my father, during the late 1930's and early 1940's, many of the looms were still powered by leather belts coming down from a revolving metal shaft attached to the ceiling. By the 1950s when I was working at the mill, the leather belts were practically eliminated, and superseded by individual electric motors bolted to the floor, one for each loom. I worked on these individually powered looms but that comes later. I was told that the individually powered looms were more efficient and cost effective than the old belt-driven looms. The old looms invariably bled power due to friction, causing uneven loom operation.

When I first visited the mill with my father the weaving

rooms were fully occupied with workers and running at or near full capacity. This was certainly the case during the World War II period (1941 to 1945). Later, when I worked in the mill in the early 1950s, the mill was operating in increasing increments below full capacity, and many weaving rooms were quiet, unlit, unheated and unoccupied. Dust collected on top of the loom frames, on warps and belts, on harnesses and dobby heads, on every horizontal and diagonal surface, everywhere.

These weaving rooms were sad and depressing to visit, like a party with a table set and decorations in place but no guests. The machinery stood ready to be started up whenever business orders would dictate, but there were no business orders coming in. When I asked when there would be business, the answers were always pessimistic, with shrugs, rolling eyeballs, and body language telling all. It was never going to happen, but people did not like to say this out loud and answered in barely audible and mumbled tones, evasively. Cold, quiet, unoccupied weaving rooms denoted an increasingly non-operating factory, with unemployed workers ready and willing to work, but with no work to be done and no pay to be earned for themselves and their families.

During the earlier years on my walks with my father, the mill was up and running full tilt, with two shifts and a partial or full third shift in operation. Of course these were happier times. There was a marvelous unmistakable clatter in the room full of running looms, and I remember that noise and din well. It would have meant nothing without the noise. I remember the shuttles going back and forth, bang, bang, bang. There was a rhythm to the weavers gliding side to side and back and forth, tending to some thirty-two looms each or so I recall. They were like dancers dancing the electric slide! With thirty-two looms to operate they had quite a large territory to cover. Paid by the piece (the number of pics per shift was the measure of product made), each weaver punched a counter at the start of each shift for each loom, which when read at the end of the shift recorded the number of pics woven that shift. The weaver coming to work for the next shift repeated the process and so cloth was made round-the-clock or almost round-the-clock. The weavers came and went each shift, but the looms ran on continuously until the last shift of the week ended late on Saturday.

Looms had auto-stops installed so that if a thread on the warp broke, a metal threadle which was suspended on that thread dropped down and activated the ever-ready back and forth check mechanism to stop the loom. With her or his hooked tool, a weaver's hook made in the machine shop in endless supply, the weaver would retrieve the broken thread, tie it using a weaver's knot to a short piece of thread pulled from a bunch of thread ends attached conveniently nearby on the top of the loom frame just for this linking purpose. Then the weaver would thread the end back through the threadle, the harness, and the reed, and then reattach the thread to the other end, all done quick as can be. Then the weaver would reposition the reed rocker in one direction or the other, locate and place the shuttle at one end, and restart the loom.

A second auto-stop mechanism assured that the loom would be stopped automatically if the thread on the bobbin in the shuttle ran out and either a new bobbin full of thread did not get inserted into the shuttle for some reason or the battery of spare full bobbins had been depleted and the battery hand had not been around to fill the battery again soon enough. A piece of metal wire of coat hanger diameter would move in and out of a cutout slot on the side of the shuttle with each pass of the shuttle, feeling to assure that there was thread on the bobbin. If the feeler wire pointing straight ahead felt the thread nothing would happen. However, if the shuttle was empty the feeler wire would contact bare wood and slide to the side. This slide would trigger the stop mechanism, requiring the weaver to remove the empty bobbin to a metal can below, take a new bobbin with thread and insert it into the shuttle, unwind some thread through the eye of the shuttle, replace the shuttle with full bobbin back into the loom at one end or the other, and restart.

This process of tending some thirty or so looms, making sure all of them were operating most of the time, restarting those which had stopped as described above, and calling the loom fixer for changeovers when the warp had been emptied and a full bolt of cloth needed to be taken away or when there were serious problems with the loom, went on for the full shift of eight hours or so, day in and day out, year in and year out, for a weaver's work lifetime. I remember meeting workers who had been employed as weavers for years. There was a real skill here.

There were always other factors that affected the efficiency of the weaving process, such as delays in fixing looms or making changeovers appropriately, epidemics of breaking threads due to environmental factors in the mill (humidity, for example), or even the presence of warp threads or filling which were below par in quality for some reason not yet attended to satisfactorily. Quality control of thread and filling was constant, and steam was jetted into the rooms to maintain proper humidity. Nevertheless, this was an endless fine-tuning process requiring close attention. Also, the mill was at pains to assure that threads and filling were of proper weight to produce the contractually specified quality of cloth. Too heavy and the finished cloth would be heavier than specified, utilizing more cotton than planned and cutting into profits. Too light and the finished cloth would be of inferior quality to what was designed, creating a contractual issue with the customer and sometimes causing extensive interruptions in the manufacturing process. This was always a subject of discussion when my father and the supervisors of the spinning room were guiding me through the intricacies of manufacturing cloth. Yet despite the vagaries of textile technology and engineering, everybody knew who the best weavers were because they consistently made more money than the others.

While I toured the mill with my father, weavers he knew would stop and talk while simultaneously tending their looms. We would slowly follow them around while they tied up broken threads and restarted the looms. All the while my father would be cautioning me to stay out of the way and not interrupt their workflow. Of course, if I did it would be detrimental to both the weaver and the mill due to lost production. But sometimes they would stop a machine anyway to show me how it worked. Sometimes they would have me move the start lever and the loom would lurch into noisy operation right before me a foot away. They would almost always take a piece of thread from the supply bunch attached to the top of the frame and tie me a weaver's knot. Then they would show me again, then have me try it while placing their hands on my small clumsy fingers, then have me try it several more times until slowly I had managed to tie a too loose, but otherwise satisfactory weaver's knot, which I promptly forgot how to do until the next time.

Then, when we approached a truly stopped machine, the weaver would drape me over the take-up cloth roll and lead me through the repair/restart process all the while talking to me and my father and moving around keeping an eye out for all the other looms under her or his care. The weaver would alight here and there like a butterfly, seemingly seeing everything to the front and the side and behind. I do believe that weavers had eyes in the back of their heads. They seemed to be able to hear the silence of a stopped loom as well as see one despite the noisy din in the weaving room. Mid-sentence, they would stop talking for a moment, reverse direction and tend to a quiet loom behind them. Their eyes and ears were ever on alert and their hands and feet ever on the move as they gracefully but gainfully wove cloth. What manual dexterity, what patience, what endurance, what perspicacity!

It was hard to hold a conversation in a weaving room or in any of the noisy production areas for that matter. Usually I saw workers talk right into somebody's ear and then turn their ear to the person's mouth to hear the reply. When calling to get the attention of somebody standing a ways away, a worker would use a falsetto voice. This higher pitch would penetrate the noisy din and be more readily heard and understood than just shouting. I would hear a "Yo" in a falsetto and look to see a person across the room respond. The ubiquitous youthful greeting of "Yo" as in "Yo, what's up?" that one may hear in the contemporary urban scene would have worked wonders in the weaving rooms of yore, just as it does today in flagging down a New York City taxi!

I do not recall anyone wearing earplugs, but maybe some did, or perhaps some workers stuffed cotton into their ears. I suspect thousands of factory workers like weavers who spent their lifetimes tending noisy machinery suffered hearing loss in later life. Today the Boott Mills, or part of it, is in the Lowell National Historical Park, and a room full of looms has been set up as an exhibit. The loom exhibit is in a small space with perhaps twenty-five to thirty looms operating on any given visiting day. This is enough to show how cloth is made, how looms were set up in rows in a large weaving room, and the noise created by a room full of looms. The National Park Service provides earplugs and urges their use. There are signs everywhere. I understand their concern, a reasonable precaution surely, but I felt like such a jerk putting them in my ears for all of five minutes worth when for all those years long past, so many thousands of textile workers toiled away with nary a thought for the damage being done incrementally and cumulatively to their hearing.

6. FLOODS.

The Merrimack River was prone to flooding, not every year, but often enough to be of concern. Even a moderate flood was newsworthy if the water level rose high enough to threaten the lower floors of the buildings along the river's edge. Newspapers and radio (WLLH) reports would bring into our home the progress of the flood waters cascading down from the Merrimack River watershed up north, and especially from Lake Winnipesaukee, the source of the Merrimack. The reports would detail the rising water measurements in Lowell and then for points upriver, providing a forecast of what was to come in the next few days. The water that was upriver had only one path to follow to the sea and the city of Lowell was on that path.

Sometimes my father would pack us into the car and we would go out to look at the high water. He would drive to and cross over the Pawtucket Street bridge above where the Lowell Textile School was located (now part of the University of Lowell) so we could see the dam upriver of the canals. At this point the dam may have been submerged, or if not it seemed to be leaking profusely between the vertical boards which constituted its top. The leaking boards gave the dam the appearance of always falling down, and maybe it was.

Following the river, we would drive down the Pawtucket side on what today is the VFW Highway to Bridge Street, all the while looking back at the city of Lowell sitting so peacefully yet vulnerably in the path of possible catastrophe. We children, however many of us went out on a trip to see the flood water, three, four, or all five of us, would never seem to get enough of the boiling, crashing high water. We would get my father to turn around and go back up to the Pawtucket Bridge again and repeat the trip. When we got to the point across from Boott Mills, he would drive across the Merrimack River on the Bridge Street bridge, then turn left onto East Merrimack Street and cross the bridge by the mouth of the Concord River where it joins the Merrimack. All of these bridges provided good flood water watching, and I remember seeing the water flowing not that many feet below the roadway. Finally, on the way home, somewhere around St. John's Hospital or perhaps it was at Andover Street, he would stop at a clear viewing site below the city to let us see the river water rushing over a small set of rapids on its way to Lawrence.

Throughout this trip, my father would be talking about the flood and what it could cause in lost production if the water kept on rising. It was exciting to experience the drama of the flood rising from a river out of control since nobody was able to predict when the crest might be reached and the river start to recede. Yet when this point was reached, everyone seemed to offer one collective community sigh of relief. I know my father did.

On March 19, 1936, a series of natural events coming together at the same time produced the flood of a century. A stormy winter with lots of snow, a spring thaw that lasted too long without the intermittent cold spells which in most years allowed for a gradual melting of the snow, and a heavy rainstorm combined to produce a dangerous flood water situation in the Merrimack River basin up north. All of this water was coming down from New Hampshire to the communities below ready or not. Great damage was caused along the way, city by city, from Manchester and Nashua, New Hampshire to Lowell, Lawrence, and Haverhill, Massachusetts, and finally out to the Atlantic Ocean at Newburyport. All locales along the way and in between these cities were inundated with high water. The first floors of the Boott Mills buildings at the river's edge were completely flooded.

The dam of the city created a reservoir of water in normal times from which the two main canals siphoned off water above the falls which when it flowed through the water wheels of the mills and back to the river below the city would have dropped some thirty-two feet. It was the water power that could be produced from this drop in the river of thirty-two feet (the "head") as it made the large bend at then East Chelmsford, that led the wealthy investors in Boston, the Boston Associates, and their cohort engineers and machinists to establish the textile manufacturing complex in 1822 that a few years later would become the city of Lowell. Kirk Boott, for whom the Boott Mills was named, was one of these early pioneer experts (see Appendix I).

Today Lowell is often cited by scholars as the birthplace of the industrial revolution in America. A number of factors contributed to this: the "mill girls" who came from the surrounding farms, and later the thousands of immigrant workers who tended the mills; the unions which organized and negotiated living wages and better work conditions; the managers who ran these mills well or less well depending on the time and the business conditions they faced and the amount of profits they sought for their stockholders; and the myriad diverse cultures that obtained around the original "mill family" over the years. A plethora of varying opinions and historical conclusions have been stated from all of these developments and because of them, the Lowell National Historical Park was created in 1978 through the leadership of the late senator Paul Tsongas, a son of Lowell. Because of the canals that were built over the ensuing twenty-six years (from 1822 to 1848), to deliver controlled water to some ten mills and a central machine shop, Lowell also has been called the "Venice of America." Indeed, Lowell is a labyrinth of canals. Every now and then a canal would be drained and I could see how deep they were and what they were made of. Old rubber automobile tires and other junk usually littered the bottoms. Every so often someone would fall into a canal and drown. In winter when it was cold enough, the canals froze and looked like wonderful places to skate, like the Hans Brinker canals in Holland. However, skating was treacherous because the moving water underneath the ice made for hazardous conditions. Drownings were reported in the winter. I recall that several boys had been skating on the surface and broke through the thin ice and drowned. My father always cautioned us never to enter a canal, not in any season of the year.

At the time the last canal was completed (1848), the chief engineer of locks and canals, James B. Francis, oversaw the design and construction of a guard gate on the original main canal to protect the city from being inundated by flood water.

This gate, now called the Francis Gate, has served its purpose twice, first in 1852 and then in 1936.

My father used to tell us that there was a question about whether, in 1936, the gate would really work since it had not been tested and lowered since 1852. However, when the decision was made it was lowered as designed with ease, and once again the city of Lowell was saved.

This gate, approximately twenty-five feet high and twenty-seven feet wide, is an awe-inspiring structure set above and between the granite walls of the canal. Today, National Park tour boats wend their way under the gate during the summer months filled with happy tourists. The gate is no longer necessary due to a series of dams built upriver, but these developments get ahead of our story.

During one of the floods, my father drove us down East Merrimack Street heading towards the center of Lowell, but we could only go as far as the Lowell Memorial Auditorium because of the high water on the Concord River and the canal. These both came together just to the south of East Merrimack Street. On the east side of the Concord River at the bridge was a low building housing Dillons, a dry cleaning establishment, This building is still there, right across from the Middlesex Community College, and it was half under water.

By the East Merrimack Street bridge, the water came over the street, which was closed to traffic, and there were waves, perhaps a foot high, rolling over towards a memorial artillery piece located on the west side of the auditorium. My father parked the car up East Merrimack Street and we walked back to play in the waves for a few minutes. We compared these waves to those we played in at the beach in Gloucester in the summer.

As my father drove around, he talked about the flood being bad for Lowell, bad for the Boott Mills, and bad for business, because of the loss of production and the yet unknown but potentially severe damage to plant and machinery. Only when the flood waters receded would the extent of damage and loss be known.

These spring floods were always a potential emergency each year, but on September 21, 1938, a hurricane sped up the Atlantic Coast at night while everyone slept, lambasting New England with huge force. I remember hearing the winds blowing all that night, and we lost electricity. I remember getting up the next morning and seeing that a big tree by the mailbox on the corner of Mansur and Fairmount Streets was down, blocking traffic coming up the hill. I remember that a big tree at the back of our house on Wyman Street had fallen over the stone wall into our yard, demolishing about ten feet of wall, which a stonemason later came to rebuild. Branches were strewn all around our house and we lost a couple of apple trees.

In the neighborhood, trees and utility poles were down everywhere, and electric and telephone wires were draped alongside and across streets. We wanted to go outside and play around the damage but because of the possible danger we were not allowed out. Over the next two to three weeks work crews arrived to cut and carry away the downed trees and restring electric and telephone wires to the poles to restore service. It was high entertainment to watch the men at work, and neighborhood groups gathered and watched with schoolroom concentration as large trees became so many manageable logs right before our eyes.

September 1938 had already been a bad month as far as floods were concerned, with rainfall measured at more than twice normal. Prior to the hurricane, New England's rivers had been swollen by four days of rain. On September 22, 1938, the day after the hurricane hit Lowell, water crossed the Pawtucket Boulevard (the VFW Highway today). The National Guard was called out, and the Locks and Canals Department requested, "All mill men on the river banks to remove articles from the lower floors." The rooms in the mill where power was generated were on the lower floors and they were flooded. Workers who reported to work were told that the high water forced the closing down of mill production and were sent home. Dillon's, the dry cleaners on East Merrimack Street at the Concord River had nine feet of water inside the building.

The water at the Pawtucket Dam was more than ninety-four feet above sea level and over sixty-two feet at the Boott Mills. The Merrimack River was thus so high that the adjoining Concord River had no place to dump its water and it too backed up and flooded East Merrimack Street, closing this street to all traffic.

The hurricane proceeded north to finally peter out in Canada, but not before dumping many inches of rain along the way in New Hampshire. This water then flooded down the Merrimack River, which ran through the riverside buildings of the Boott Mills for several days. I remember seeing chicken coops floating by, and large trees and numerous branches and telephone poles. The river flowed quickly and there were rough waves to be seen. When the low water months arrived the next summer exposing the jagged rock bottom of the river bed in front of the Boott Mills, I remember seeing an old car at rest, having been rolled that far by the raging waters of the previous fall flood.

While it is conceivable that I am remembering the 1936 flood, I am not sure since I would have been less than three years old. However, by the 1938 flood I would have been more than five years old and I remember it accurately. I think that I was told a great deal about the 1936 flood, but was told about and personally experienced the 1938 hurricane and resulting flood.

My father took me to the mill for one of our visits during the 1938 flood at a time when the Merrimack River included the Boott Mills in its stream. That is, the river flowed through the mill for several days. We were on an upper floor, looking down through a stairwell while talking to some men on duty, and all I could see below was muddy water flowing over the tops of machinery, except that sandbags surrounded one specialty machine which appeared to be dry. The water must have been some four to five feet deep on the floor below as it flowed out through the windows at the downstream end. After the river receded, I recall a report that workers had found a telephone pole in the mill and some chicken coops with dead birds in them. Also, there were mounds of mud and sand left behind which had to be shoveled out the now vacant window openings to the river bank below or hauled out in wheel barrows to the mill yard. Much manual labor had to be expended before the mechanics could attempt to clean, repair, and restart the machinery and resume production.

My father prided himself on getting the mill back and

running as soon as possible after one of these devastating catastrophic events. Of course, doing so was good for business and good for the workers' morale and pocketbooks, but it was more than that. It was that he felt a personal responsibility to the city of Lowell and its economy and communal well-being. He had terrible pride about this, and it drove him to do everything possible to get the Boott Mills back into normal production before any of the other mills in the city. He was quite competitive about this, always wanting the Boott Mills to be the first mill back on line, which it usually was.

It is family lore that after the 1936 flood, he drove around Lowell to every hardware store and bought them out of all the shovels and brooms they had which he loaded in the backseat and trunk of his car and personally delivered to the mill. Until the mud and debris left from the flood were removed, there could be no production. Workers who could not at first work on textile production were reassigned if they agreed to join the maintenance cleanup crews and help out. Extra brooms and shovels, indeed a good supply of them, were necessary if these extra hands were to be effective at digging and sweeping. They would also get paid sooner than they anticipated after the flood if they accepted the maintenance clean-up work. My father was ready for them and dig, sweep and clean up many of them did. The Boott Mills was the first mill back on line in the city. My father told this story often, and after he died my mother carried on by telling this story often too.

The Boott Mills by my time had long since converted the water power from powering a direct mechanical linkage of gears and shafts to run machinery, to powering its own power-producing generators. These generators in turn powered electric motors that ran the machinery. The mill also had installed coal-fired steam boilers to produce steam for generating electricity when water power in the dry months was insufficient. Finally, the mill purchased electricity from the local electric company. Large cable electric wires coming in over the roof delivered the purchased electricity. Most of the other mills that bought power used underground wires which my father said were better protected from the elements than above-ground wires, except in the case of flood threat when underground cables were vulnerable. My father believed the Boott Mills had used the proper foresight in opting for above-ground electric service versus underground delivery. Clearly there were pros and cons here, trade-offs, but my father believed the Boott had gotten it right and could call on water power, steam-generated power, or local electric company power in one combination or another for its electricity needs, whichever was most cost effective at the time.

Fuel supply during World War II was an on-going issue and everybody worried about having enough, especially during the cold months. We burned coal at home and I will remember forever the horrible taste of coal dust and the smell of it in the house, and the crinkly sound of coal grains underfoot upstairs even though the furnace and coal bin were in the basement. Our cat used to use the coal bin to crap in rather than face the cold and snow outside and would come upstairs looking filthy. Meanwhile the coal bin used to stink something awful. Some of my friends lived in more modern houses heated by cleaner oil, and I vowed if ever given the choice I would choose oil. I saw both oil and coal trucks in the neighborhood, and told myself that the oil trucks were better. Despite my antipathy to coal, it was great fun to watch the two men deliver it by hand. One heavy canvas coal tote bag at a time was filled to the brim from a chute at the back of the coal truck and carried to an opened basement window to be dumped into the coal bin below. Back and forth they went many times until the ordered amount had been physically transported. Now this was hard work! The coal men were characters with tattoos and salty language and always had dirty faces and clothes. They joked with us while doing their jobs. They complained about the cat crap stink and told us to keep the damn cat out of the coal. But at the Boott Mills the coal supply was no light issue and pains were taken to assure there was always a good supply on hand, for assuring steady war production demanded no less.

Along the French and John Street parking lots in front of the mill where the railroad siding that was used to bring the cotton in was located, there were huge piles of coal, the coal also coming by rail. These piles at times were as high as a two or three-story building. As the supply was used up the pile would shrink, and soon it would be time to restock. My father liked the look of the huge piles of coal in front of the mill, just one less thing to worry about.

My Uncle Frederick used to take a drive to New Hampshire every spring to check the water levels upriver so he could calculate how long water power could be used and how much coal would need to be bought. As long as the coal piles existed at street side, a night watchman was posted nearby to guard against pilferage. This huge supply of coal was enticing in a war time, energy-rationed economy.

The spring floods on the Merrimack River were an annual threat to the city of Lowell, and there was little anybody could do about it. There was always talk about flood control but that would mean building expensive dams in New Hampshire for which there was insufficient political support. Finally, after World War II, flood control gained sufficient attention and political support to become a reality. The U.S. Army Corps of Engineers conducted studies that resulted in a plan to build several dams in New Hampshire which would finally eliminate the annual risk of floods. Congresswoman Edith Nourse Rogers, also my "Aunt Edith," represented the fifth district in Congress in which Lowell was located since 1925. She succeeded her husband John Jacob Rogers who had died in office, and she fought tirelessly for flood control on the Merrimack River throughout her career.

One summer in the late 1940s while our family was driving through New Hampshire on vacation, my father left the main road and went past a detour sign on to an old narrow road that took us down a steep hill. My mother protested all the way down, asking my father where on earth he thought he was going. My mother had a way of confronting my father like this, but when he was determined it was all to no avail; he obviously was on a mission and knew exactly what he was about. Soon we were at the bottom of the hill and entering a small village nestled by the Merrimack River, and what a sight we saw. There were homes, schools, churches, stores, everything you would expect to find in a small village anywhere, only here some of the buildings were up on blocks ready to be moved out. Everywhere there were empty foundations from which buildings had been removed. Further on were buildings not yet reached by the movers, but they were ready to be moved. Safety lines were up and perimeters were cleared of debris and vegetation. These buildings would be next in line to be jacked up, blocked, and then moved away on flatbeds. There were no people around and it was eerie. The people had long since left, and we were visiting on an off day for the movers.

A new location for the village had been selected and those buildings that could be moved were moved uphill to it. In due course the dams were built, the old village flooded out, and the mayhem of the spring floods a happening of the past never to be repeated again. Several years later, while driving through New Hampshire we drove by one of the new dams with a large lake formed above it and saw a trickle of water flowing below the dam into the reconstituted Merrimack River.

Years later, in 1970, the Boott Mills having ceased operations in 1954 and my father having retired at last from a second job as a vice president for purchasing at Samson Ocean Systems, Inc., Massachusetts governor Francis Sargent appointed him to the board of directors of the Merrimack Valley Flood Control Authority, and he was reappointed after that. He was proud to be associated with this government authority. He had talked about flood control at home for years, advocated it professionally when given the opportunity, and witnessed firsthand the devastation floods caused to textile production in Lowell, to the Lowell economy, and to the community at large. His feelings and beliefs would extend as well to all the other cities and towns up and down the Merrimack River which suffered flood devastation comparable to Lowell's. Of course these communities like Lowell had benefited most of the time from the five hundred-foot drop between Lake Winnipesaukee and the Atlantic Ocean which created the water power and thus their livelihood for many years. Nevertheless, they paid for it big time at flood time when the Merrimack River raged out of control.

7. GROWING UP IN A MILL MANAGER'S FAMILY.

My father worked a five and a half day week just as all the other mill employees did. In other words, the mill operated on Saturdays, and he was there for half a day. Later, when the mill cut back and did not operate on Saturdays my father went to work on Saturdays for half a day. That was my father. At age fifty-seven he began work for Samson Ocean Systems in Boston, and it was the first time in his life that he did not work on Saturdays. For a while he almost did not know what to do with himself on Saturday mornings.

The typical day for my father began when he left the house on foot about 7:30 a.m. in the morning and walked down Mansur Street to Nesmith Street. Then he walked down East Merrimack Street to "the square," and then along Bridge Street to French Street to John Street. (The mill was at the foot of John Street.) The walk was about a mile and it took him about fifteen minutes. At noon, if he did not have a business meeting downtown, he would walk home for a quick lunch of soup and sandwiches and walk back after lunch, another two miles round trip.

At 5:00 p.m. or so he would leave the mill and walk the mile home up the gentle slope of East Merrimack Street. Total exercise for the day, one hour; total distance walked, four miles. He liked this form of exercise and his physical appearance reflected it. As a young man he had played some golf, but had long since given it up because it cut into his family life.

Years later as a senior citizen, when he attended some Boy Scout and veterans' events, he wore with pride his Boy Scout's "Life and Star Scout" uniform, last worn when he was fifteen or sixteen years old, and his World War I U.S. Army uniform, last worn when he was eighteen. Both uniforms were a slight squeeze for him to get into and he mildly complained about having gained too much weight. My reaction to that was yeah, give me a break! At most he had gained five pounds in fifty years, but he could still button his pants.

His male neighbors customarily drove to work each day more or less the same distance he walked. He used to say that when he first started to work they would stop to offer him a ride, but they soon understood he would never accept it, and they would drive by with a wave and a toot. This occurred rain or shine, year round, for his entire work life in Lowell.

In addition to walking he practiced simple eating habits, not because he was trying to maintain or meet any particular health standard or medical prescription, but merely by personal choice. He ate five prunes, oatmeal, and one piece of toast for breakfast his whole life. Lunch was typically soup and a sandwich. Dinner would be the usual meat or fish, vegetable and potato or rice combination, with fruit for dessert, or on special occasions Indian pudding. He loved Indian pudding. I don't recall him eating seconds and he did not like ice cream. What a father! How can you not like ice cream?

Alcoholic beverages were minimal, and never consumed

other than at special occasions like parties or weddings. He never had a cocktail hour and early in their marriage, my mother and he dropped out of a neighborhood cocktail hour set. They rarely socialized, living a life devoted to their chosen role as parents of five children. During World War II a sixth child was added through their joining an exchange program that brought children fleeing the bombings over from England. Norman Davey joined the family in 1940 at the age of seven and lived with us until his return to England in 1944 at age eleven.

I used to wonder if my parents had any friends. They did, but they just did not get to see them very often when we were growing up. The family was everything.

My father liked to smoke a pipe in his early years, but he gave that up too.

My father lived a serious, cautious, conservative life and what mattered to him mattered deeply. First and foremost was his wife and his children; family mattered. Second was Lowell. He was born, bred, worked, died and buried in Lowell. His city mattered passionately. He used to talk about the importance of his family and his city to him. Thereafter, depending on the context, his mill (the Boott Mills), his college (Harvard), and his church (then the All Souls Church, but now Christ Church United) mattered. He was active on a number of boards in Lowell as was my mother, and community service took virtually all of their spare time. I never knew my father to decline serving on a board of a local service organization. If anything cut into their role as parents beyond my father's work commitment to the mill, it was community service. Community service in Lowell for my father was an extension of his devotion to the city and a desire to make it better by helping those less well off. He also wanted to help institutions in the city, such as the Lowell General Hospital, that existed to serve everybody. My mother, an active Girl Scout leader when she met my father, joined him in a mutually shared commitment to Lowell. She had an array of activities in organizations that were always focused on enhancing the health and well-being of women, girls, and children.

She was active in the Girl Scouts, Lowell Arts Club, YWCA, Florence Crittendon League, and St. Joseph's Hospital School of Nursing. She made an easy transition from Brookline, where she grew up to Lowell as a result of her seven plus years organizing and leading Girl Scout troops in Lynn prior to her marriage at age twenty-five and move to Lowell. Lynn was not all that different a city from Lowell only Lynn made shoes while Lowell made cotton cloth. The girls who joined the Girl Scouts were the blue-collar shoe workers' daughters. She also was a Girl Scout leader in the South End of Boston and served as a member of the board of directors of the South End Settlement House for many years. She also worked on Boy Scout affairs when her sons were involved. I was a member of the Immaculate Conception Church Cub Scout troop for three years while my mother served as my den mother.

My family was close knit across generations, with my two paternal grandparents and my maternal grandmother figuring prominently in our growing up and my parents' activities after that. My maternal grandfather had died of the flu in 1918 during the terrible epidemic that took thousands of lives across the United States, but not before as a licensed surveyor, he had surveyed the lot on which Fenway Park was built in 1912. My mother fondly remembered seeing the Boston Red Sox play at the old Huntington Avenue Fair Grounds and the new Fenway Park. She was a lifelong Red Sox fan, even more so than my father, and they both watched most of the Red Sox games on television in their senior years.

My father visited his parents next door just about every evening and sometimes this would extend into the family dinner hour much to the consternation of my mother. Living next door, we saw my paternal grandparents all the time. My mother's mother, widowed as noted above, lived about an hour away in Brookline, Massachusetts. We would see her on numerous weekends and holidays making trips to Brookline in the winter and Gloucester in the summer where she had a summer house. My father took two weeks of vacation a year and my maternal grandmother usually joined us for the family vacation.

8. JUST ONE MORE THING.

As previously noted, during the summer months, we frequently spent the weekend in Gloucester, Massachusetts with my grandmother. On Saturdays, my father would go to work while my mother would get us five or six kids up, fed, bathed, dressed, and packed for the trip. Just before noon we would load into the car and my mother would drive down to the mill. There we would park in the hot sun in the mill parking lot by a mill building long since torn down and wait for my father's expected immediate arrival. This was all done according to an explicit schedule and plan discussed by my parents earlier, but we would wait and wait. The minutes ticked by and noon would become 12:15, 12:20, and stuffed into a hot car, we children would become restless and whiney. We still had over an hour's ride to Gloucester.

Soon enough, my mother would take action. She would turn toward me and say "Rog, go rouse out your father," and I would proceed to do so.

A canal flowed right in front of the mill, like a castle moat. There was a vehicle bridge on the left side, slanting down over the canal to the mill yard below. There were three parallel rows of red brick buildings between the canal and the river, with a large mill yard between the first and second rows, and a space between the second and third rows. The often photographed clock tower with the shuttle weather vane is located on one side of the large mill yard, attached to the middle or second row of buildings.

Just to the right of this wide vehicle bridge was a footwalk bridge that went straight across the canal to the second floor of a two-story mill building called the Counting House which housed the administrative and management offices. My father's office was here, where I had ostensibly blown out the telephone system of the mill in my earlier visit. He shared the office with his brother, my uncle Frederick. Today, this two-story building houses some of the administrative offices and exhibits of the Boott Cotton Mills Museum.

So after my mother told me to go rouse out my father, I would get out of the car and cross the gravel parking lot. I remember the parking lot was first paved with boiler cinders from burnt coal but later was upgraded to a macadam surface. During World War II, across the parking lot by the railroad siding were huge hills of coal, perhaps thirty to forty feet high. I would cross the footbridge, find my way to his office, and "rouse out my father." My mere presence was all that this came to, a messenger boy. He would mumble something like, "Just one more thing." And I would retrace my steps back to the car and tell my mother and my siblings that he was coming. But we would sit and wait, sit and wait some more.

Ten, fifteen minutes would pass. We children would grow restless. My mother would become more perturbed, and soon I would be dispatched again to go rouse out my father, only this time her voice would be harsh to me as if I were the one at fault. Maybe I was meant to carry her harshness to him somehow.

I would mildly complain, feeling the pressure on a child caught between two parents in conflict. My mere presence underscored their lack of agreement on when a manager's workday properly finishes, and neither seemed to want to see me. My presence at the door to my father's office communicated my mother's growing wrath, and nobody who had ever witnessed my mother's wrath would knowingly encounter it again given a choice. My presence back at the car, alone without my father in sight, reinforced in my mother's mind, my father's over preoccupation with work and under appreciation of his family responsibilities. The "just one more thing" refrain had no supportable basis on a Saturday when the family was waiting to go to Gloucester, World War II or no World War II.

When he finally arrived, looking hassled and preoccupied, he would have the look of a defeated man. He knew what was coming next. She would lace into him something fierce. "What do you think you are doing? What were you thinking, making these children wait for you out here in the hot sun while you do just one more thing? These children want to go to Gloucester and we are going to go to Gloucester". He never said anything I could hear beyond a few mumbles. He had no excuses and he made none. It didn't matter what he said at that point anyway. On Saturdays, he dressed the way he always did on any other work day. suit and tie, never a sport coat, and his hat. He would get in, shed his suit coat and hat, take the wheel, and we would be off to Gloucester in silence. My parents didn't speak and we children were fearful of doing so, until somebody felt carsick or needed a bathroom stop.

I was the only person who could rouse out my father. My brother was too young and my sisters were not allowed in the mill. Family management, family women, that is Flather family women, were not allowed in the mill. There was no law, just family rule or custom. No Flather women in the mill, ever! This annoyed my sisters, especially Allie, who was closest in age to me and who was always competing with me and feeling slighted. My oldest sister Kitsey did not worry about such things and my younger sister Betsey was too young to worry about it at all.

I was the only one and I knew the rule, so when I complained to my mother and procrastinated, I was really finding an excuse to put down my sisters I suppose. "Why does he get to go? Why is he the only one? I want to see Dad's office too," my sister Allie would complain to no avail. My mother had never been inside the mill either nor had my grandmother. My mother did not bother to explain. She would just tell Allie to be quiet and thus accept her lot as a Flather female.

Years later, when the mill was near closing and Allie was a good deal older, she managed to convince my father to show her his office. Betsey also got to see the office before the mill closed for good in 1954, but alas they never had the opportunity to be out on the production floors where the cloth was made.

PART 2: THE WAR YEARS AND AFTERMATH (1940s)

9. THE ARMY-NAVY E.

The first Army-Navy E Production Award, more familiarly known as the Army-Navy "E" (Excellence) award, was given to an ordnance manufacturer in August 1941, even before Pearl Harbor. The Boott's award was the first given to a New England cotton mill, and by war's end, the Boott Mills was the only cotton mill in the United States to have received four stars on the Army-Navy E pennant.

On October 1, 1942, less than a year after the Pearl Harbor attack and the start of World War II, the Boott Mills was awarded its first Army-Navy E (Excellence) Pennant. By that time, it had been producing khaki for the army whites and khaki for the navy and for a short while greys for the naval officer uniforms until the navy changed its mind and discontinued the grey uniforms.

Near the end of 1938, the Boott Mills won a small contract to produce eight thousand yards of uniform material for the Navy. This quantity was substantially increased in 1939, doubled in 1940, doubled again in 1941. Thus the Boott Mills was well on its way to wartime production even before December 7, 1941, Pearl Harbor. In 1942 after eight months, the volume had been increased to fourteen million yards which was double that of 1941.

The government had three criteria for winning the award:

1. That the firm had volunteered to do Navy work before Pearl Harbor.
2. That close to 100% of production was on government work.
3. That the firm had done something outstanding and unique, on its own, for the war effort. In the case of the Boott Mills a training school had been established to train workers for textile employment and the resulting training manual had been distributed nationwide by the War Production Board.

There was to be a ceremony in the mill yard below the famous clock tower with the shuttle weather vane. An admiral and other senior military officers would be in attendance. Also, Congresswoman Edith Nurse Rogers (Republican, Massachusetts 5th District, and my Aunt Edith), and all manner of local dignitaries, including the lieutenant governor of Massachusetts and the mayor of Lowell, would be there. Key employees and supervisors would be assigned special seats, and of course the board of directors would receive special accommodations. This was a proud and patriotic time, and my father, leading up to it, was ever so proud and excited. What mattered to him, family, mill, city, and patriotic recognition, were all rolled up into one fabulous event.

A bandstand was built for the dignitaries and decorated with red, white and blue bunting, and a special flagpole installed in the mill yard on which to raise the Army-Navy E during the ceremony. Several female employees were selected to raise the pennant. Later, Army-Navy E lapel pennant pins were distributed to all employees and guests. The Army-Navy E pennant would fly high over the mill, just below the American flag for the balance of the war. Beyond, facing the band stand was the assembled work force, perhaps a thousand or two workers.

The Flather family male only rule still applied, but there had to be a way found for Flather women to attend. The executive offices lined one side of the mill yard and arrangements were made for the Flather women to sit by the windows on the second floor and look out over the proceedings. When Flather family women entered the mill for the first time on October 1, 1942, they did so by crossing the footbridge to the second floor of the executive offices. They were still separated from production areas of the mill, including the mill yard and production people male and female.

I, being male, was treated differently, as I always had been when it came to the mill. I was down with my father in the bandstand with the dignitaries no less and meeting the admiral. After the ceremony I milled about with my two male cousins, Fred III and Charles who also was privileged that day and seated in the bandstand with his father Frederick Junior. The three of us were treated preferentially as Flather men while our collective sisters were given inferior status.

I remember looking up and seeing my grandmother, my aunt May (my grandmother's sister), my mother, my other aunt Edith, wife of my uncle Frederick, my sisters Kitsey and Allie, and my cousin Edith (Fred's oldest sister).

What a day! The weather was perfect. Bands played, and speeches were made by my grandfather, father, and Uncle Frederick representing the mill, by the dignitaries representing the navy and by the local political leaders. Unfortunately,

Congresswoman Rogers was unable to attend because of pressing business in Washington much to the disappointment of my father. But the ceremony carried on just as if she had been there in all her wonderful presence. Photographs were taken and I was treated as a family VIP while my poor sisters had to watch it all as second class citizens from a second-floor window. There is a photograph of the ceremony with the executive offices in the background and barely visible is a girlish figure leaning out of one of the windows. She looks decidedly like my thirteen-year-old sister Kitsey.

Everyone in attendance, every dignitary, every guest, every worker received an Army-Navy lapel pin that day. The pin was attached to a card that stated, "Message from the President of United States. Wear your Army-Navy E award emblem with pride. Remember always that it is the symbol of your own individual contribution to the defeat of our enemies." The other side of the card said, "For skill, industry, and devotion to the production front of the greatest war in history, this Army-Navy Production Award emblem hereby presented to _____ of _____." The card included printed signatures of the president, War Department, and Navy Department officials. The Lowell National Park Museum collection contains some of these pins, as well as an original Army-Navy E pennant and many photographs, and includes them in periodic exhibits.

10. My Father's Role during World War II.

Evening was always a beautiful time to drive by the mill, especially during the war years, with three shifts operating, and especially from across the river on the Pawtucket/ Tyngsborough side. Here one could look back and see the lighted mills all along the opposite shore for as far as the eye could see, the Miracle Mile. My father loved that, and often at night, when we were on the way home from some place he would take a "wrong turn," much to the frustration of my mother, and drive by to see the Boott Mills working at night. Years later, when production slowed, when there was no third shift, then no second shift, then no shifts at all, the mill at night would be partially lit or darkened completely. It was easy to tell how the mill was doing; just drive by at night!

My father was responsible for all customer relations during the war. That is, he handled all contracts and relationships with the army and the navy. Typically this meant he traveled at least once a week throughout the war to New York, where he would visit the navy clothing depot in Brooklyn, or to Philadelphia, and/or Washington, D.C. He would go to bed early, wearing his pajamas. Then, when it was time to board the train, at 11:00 p.m. he would put his suit on over his pajamas, call a taxi and proceed to the railroad station. He would take the sleeper in Lowell which would be picked up some time during the night and hitched to a New York City bound train which would arrive at Pennsylvania Station the next morning before work. He would then complete his business and return the same way, taking a sleeper out of New York and arriving in Lowell where the sleeper was dropped off early the next morning to a siding, allowing him to go straight to the mill after he awoke.

On trips to Philadelphia and Washington, D.C. he might be away for two days. This schedule was tiring, and I remember him being a tired, that is, unavailable, father much of the time, but on occasion he would return with a present or a toy for each of us and there was great family excitement and happiness as a result.

He traveled light, usually carrying only a small leather suitcase the size of a briefcase, in which he included a change of clothes, work kit, and all his business papers. Somehow there was still room for the toys!

As I look back on the war years, I realize that my father was not away completely, like a soldier or sailor, and not in harm's way. He was still physically present as my father which could not be said for many thousands of children whose fathers were serving in the armed forces. On the other hand, the pressure on him to produce material for the army and the navy was so great that much of the time it seemed that he might as well have been away fighting because I did not feel his presence as a father. When I read that the Boott Mills became the navy's largest supplier of white uniform twill such that one out of two sailors wore uniforms made from cloth woven at the Boott Mills in Lowell, Massachusetts, I understand how hard he had to work to assure production requirements were met and that he was doing all he could to support the war effort personally.

Making 50% of all the sailors' uniforms made in World War II in just one mill in Lowell, Massachusetts while being in competitive bid situations with more cost-efficient southern mills was an incredible feat, yet this is precisely what the Boott Mills accomplished. It is little wonder that the Boott Mills was awarded the Army-Navy "E" production award followed by four more awards during the course of the war, signified each time by the addition of a star. A fifth star was scheduled to be awarded later in 1945, but the war ended first.

Early in 1942 my father brought home a poster depicting a tattered American flag and containing the caption "Remember Pearl Harbor, December 7, 1941." There followed perhaps every two weeks or so for the next two years, yet another poster supporting the war effort. These posters built patriotism with exhortations such as "Loose lips sink ships" and "Should brave men die so you can drive?" The posters were printed by the War Department, Office of War Information, and were mailed in batches nationwide to companies manufacturing supplies and equipment for the war effort.

I hung some of them on the walls of my bedroom and exchanged them as new posters were printed. After about two years, the poster program came to an end, to be replaced by biweekly war maps. These maps provided brief summaries of recent events in the major theaters of the war – the Russian front, Italy, Europe after D-Day, and the Pacific.

In my mind, the posters served to underscore the war effort as far as the Boott Mills was concerned since that is where they came from before coming to me. I believe I understood as well as a child could what my father was doing at the mill to make cloth for uniforms for our soldiers and sailors overseas.

At war's end the posters and maps were packed away in a cardboard box which moved with me many times over the next fifty years. The box was in storage, in closets, attics, basements, and under our bed. My wife Becky frequently questioned my attachment to this collection suggesting it could be disposed of, but I could not throw them away. To this day they link me to my father and the Boott Mills during the World War II period.

Finally in 1995 I took steps to find a permanent home for the posters, seeking an institution that would preserve them for posterity. I was fortunate to be placed in touch with the library of the Boston Athenaeum, which already possessed an excellent World War II poster collection and was overjoyed to be able to add my World War II collection to it. Some seventy-five items were included in the gift to the Athenaeum.

In 2008 the Athenaeum staged a spectacular exhibit of twenty-six posters and war maps including the famous "Four Freedoms" by Norman Rockwell.

11. PRESSURE ON WAGES.

During the war the Boott Mills had become unionized at the urging of the navy procurement offices and textile wages had increased. The military customers beseeched the mill management to maintain production at all cost. Labor problems and labor stoppages could not be tolerated, and were not. Management felt they were overpaying, especially the less skilled and less motivated who were hired only because of a labor scarcity with so many men away in the service and many others being siphoned off to higher paying munitions jobs at the Remington Arms plant in South Lowell. Full-page ads extolled the higher wages and benefits and patriotism in switching to Remington Arms. It was not just the textile mills that had to face this competition. Local retailers such as the department stores along Merrimack Street were also hurt, and some of these employers fought back with ads of their own to the effect that workers who went to Remington short-term for the war effort would not be rehired at war's end when there would be no call to make munitions in Lowell. For a time people seemed to talk as much about the ads, the choices, the rumors and the gossip of which people went where to work and at what pay as about the war. Ellen, our cook, talked about it in the kitchen, perhaps implying that my parents should

61

pay her more money too. With so many workers receiving war-induced pay increases, I think she felt left behind. A cook in a textile management home was part of the war effort, too, wasn't she?

At war's end in August of 1945 wartime production stopped precipitously. The Japanese officially surrendered on August 15, 1945. On August 16, 1945 the Boott Mills received a naval speed letter that stated in part, "Your contract is off immediately X Immediately stop all work Term subcontracts and place no further orders..." Production at the Boott Mills came to a screeching halt! This was just one day after the official war end.

While everyone else in the United States was justifiably celebrating victory, my father had already turned his attention to planning the transition to peace time products and sales, a mandatory requirement for the mill to survive and be profitable.

After the war, it was catch up time for America. We caught up on consumer goods like cars and refrigerators that replaced the old ice boxes, caught up on housing, caught up on wages, caught up on everything. As a child I really noticed the priority during the war for war production by going into the five and dime stores and seeing the dearth of toys and shoddy quality of those few items that were available. But after the war, wow, the stores were soon full of new toys and many were made out of that new war material called plastic, now finally made available to the consumer marketplace.

PART 3: STRIKE

PART 3: STRIKE

The end of the war in August 1945 brought the cancellation of orders from the military, and the Boott Mills had to manage a quick transition to peace time production of towels and corduroy while seeking along with just about every other business in America to make the right decisions for assuring speedy peace time profitability. Maintaining profitability in a peace time market with wartime wages was a challenge, exacerbated by the commitment of labor to also effect catch up wage increases across the board, industry by industry, nationwide. Whether war time wages had been allowed to get too high or had had the lid kept on them in support of the war effort did not matter. The labor union calls for high wage increases were based on need and reward, and carefully crafted campaigns to achieve increases for their members were the result.

The Textile Workers Union of America (TWUA) selected the Boott Mills as their pattern target, where success with the newly negotiated increases might be easily spread throughout the industry. The Boott Mills was well known for its four Army-Navy E awards and a fifth was intended once a requisite time interval had passed, but the war ended first. After each award, another star was sewn on the army-navy pennant. The Boott Mills was the only unionized mill in Lowell at this time.

The mill was struck in October 1947 and the strike was not settled until April 1948, after some eight months of work stoppage. At the time it was one of the longest strikes going on anywhere in the United States. The settlement was at or very near the terms management had offered months earlier, which needled my father to no end. "Such loss, such needless waste," he would say, while also realizing the strike was somewhat inevitable and had to run its course.

The Boott Mills was in good company. At the time, it seemed the whole country was on strike as unions in industry after industry sought new benefits and higher wages, for the most part successfully. Harry Truman was president and the industrial labor management climate became so politically charged that the Republicans in Congress were able to pass the controversial pro-management Taft-Hartley Act over the president's veto.

John L. Lewis, representing coal miners, and Walter Reuther, representing auto workers, stood out in endless press reports. Lewis, with his bushy eyebrows, long hair, and deep voice was the devil incarnate. In my house they were the enemy which led to confusion in my mind. How could such an evil man be allowed such free rein to talk and act out? Years later, after I toured Harland and Hazard counties in Eastern Kentucky and saw firsthand the poverty of mining families, I better understood the case of the United Mine Workers and John L. Lewis.

The subtleties and ambiguities of such political and economic issues were beyond a child's ability to comprehend, and I did not get any help in a management household whose adult members had long since established a pro-management

Republican point of view. There was no voice for the other side on these issues while I was growing up.

My father used to receive numerous phone calls evenings and weekends from workers who disagreed with their union's stance and wanted to return to work. These workers were likely the ones with the fewest alternatives, such as weavers, and predominantly women. Women were less union-oriented than men at that time and less mobile. Men, especially machinists and loom fixers, were more pro-union. Their skills made them more readily transferable to other technical areas, and they were certainly more mobile. It was easier for men to travel, commute, or relocate. For many of the women on strike, their choice was to have no money or to do child care and take in laundry or similar types of jobs. The men were always able to work in other textile mills or in such areas as automobile repair, seemingly without losing a beat, and sometimes even making more money.

However, the real challenge was more for the union leadership than the workers. The leaders had set themselves up to succeed and labor's eyes were on them nationwide. They had to make the good fight and it took a while for this necessary process to run its course before there could be successful negotiation. When serious, purposeful negotiations finally occurred, the settlement came quickly and was essentially what could have been agreed upon at the outset had the issues between labor and management been limited to just those applicable to that one mill in Lowell, Massachusetts. It was the national objective of using the Boott strike as a pattern for other New England textile mills and even mills nationwide that made settlement so difficult early on.

Early in the strike after the union had established daily picket lines, a delegation of Lowell police officers visited my grandfather at home one day to request that he not try to have his chauffeur-driven car cross the picket line. The police said they just wanted to take every precaution to avoid trouble.

My grandfather took their request under advisement, but the next day when he customarily went to the mill before taking the train to Boston, he instructed his chauffeur to drive slowly and cautiously as they approached the picket lines with the objective of entering the mill parking lot. As the car approached the picketers, the line parted and the men doffed their caps to my grandfather. Thereafter, he was able to drive through the parted line without incident.

On the other hand, my youngest sister Betsey remembers driving somewhere with my grandfather during the strike and being in the car when it was hit with a couple of eggs.

During the strike my oldest sister Kitsey was working at the Lowell Day Nursery, one of the organizations my mother was involved with. One day a father picking up his daughter pointedly said to Kitsey, "And where is your father working today?" She was a bit unnerved, but she replied, "He's at the mill," in as even a voice as she could manage. Nothing more was said.

Each day my father's routine remained the same. He walked to and from work, and he would say, "Good morning," and tip his hat as he passed through the picket line. There was never any trouble. This was not a strike that generated anger or outward resentment sufficient to lead to violence. It was a relatively peaceful strike at the street level throughout the eight months duration. All the tough sledding was at the negotiation table.

During the strike, the lid was on at home in terms of the behavior of us children. My father would come home tired and dejected and he would force a smile indicating that he had had a good day working in a plant without one spindle turning. My mother would keep us children out of the way and try and make a happy home life so my father could rest for his duties the next day. My father did most of the labor negotiating.

Of course I grew up in a management home. My family was Republican, pro-business, and anti-union. For the most part only the management side was ever discussed and supported, but there were ambiguities and questions and contrary voices did sneak through. If unions were so bad how could they be allowed to exist? If they were so bad how could presidents Roosevelt and Truman tolerate or support them? (Of course my family did not vote for either of them.) If unions were so bad, why did thousands of people want to join them? These questions and ambiguities for the most part were not answered or tolerated in my home, my management home.

The way I learned about the other side was through radio and *Life* magazine. Special people like federal mediators and judges seemed almost godlike, and they received considerable attention and publicity. The labor story got through and like forbidden fruit, I wanted to know more about it, but this had to wait. I was not going to be able to trade with the enemy in my father's house, and the only side I was going to hear there was the management side. My father was not rigid or doctrinaire on this issue; rather, having looked at the data and made his analysis, he had concluded that unions, while inescapably part of the landscape he had to deal with, were sometimes bad for the Boott Mills, bad for Lowell, and bad for the Flathers. It was a waste of time to be thinking otherwise about unions. End of story, at least for a while.

When I started working at the Boott Mills in July 1959, I wanted to join the union and expected to, but I was denied. Management was opposed, and the union made no fuss. I was disappointed, but the two sides were in agreement about the boss's son and I was powerless to change that. My father was not amused when I asked to join the union, and the issue was never discussed again.

My union days would finally come, first as a graduate business school student at Northeastern University in the late '50s where I took courses on labor-management and the history of unions in the United States. Second, as a New York City special education public school teacher, starting in 1987, I was privileged to be a member of the United Federation of Teachers (UFT) which continues into my retirement.

My family was conservative in other ways too. I used to think they were "square" to a fault. One time, my father came home to unwind from a personal problem at the mill which was most upsetting to him, but had to be dealt with. Rarely did mill problems cross the threshold of the family circle, but this serious one did. I think he talked about it at home with the expectation that my mother would support him and perhaps even suggest that the decision he was about to make was appropriate since she had been working for so many years as a volunteer for the Florence Crittendon League and had experience with helping unwed mothers.

The case involved one of his key supervisors, a married

man with family who had gotten one of his female subordinates pregnant. It was a management issue plain and simple as far as my father was concerned for if not dealt with correctly and quickly it would be detrimental to morale in the workplace and bring discredit upon management. If management did not establish and maintain a proper moral climate, who would? He agonized over losing a good supervisor, but in the end the supervisor was let go.

Views on morality can change from generation to generation, and Kitsey and Allie and I did not see any reason to fire the man, but my father was determined and unrelenting on this one. All of this was thrashed out after church one Sunday at lunch around the dining-room table.

My family felt important in Lowell, but I felt they felt too important and sometimes I found their actions and words embarrassing. My grandmother used to drive around Lowell sitting in the back of her chauffeured Cadillac at Christmastime, passing out envelopes of cash to selected police officers on duty at key intersections in the city. The most important of these was "the Square," right in the center where East Merrimack Street crosses Bridge Street. Before a stop light was installed, traffic at this intersection was always controlled by a patrol officer on foot. Coming through "the Square," so my father would say, if the officer saw a Flather car back in the pack, he would move the traffic through until the Flather car had passed. Then he would halt the traffic and switch to the crossing traffic. One year, my parents heard through the grapevine that one of the envelopes was mistakenly left empty of cash.

PART 4: MILL WORKER

12. My Father's Pride and Joy.

On or about July 15, 1950, my planned two and a half month long tour of the United States with good friend Jimmy Grey abruptly ended after a frenetic five weeks. We had gone coast to coast and back, had not earned a nickel en route despite having planned to live off the land, and were back home early. Been there, done that, with no plans or even thoughts about what to do for the rest of the summer.

Backing up, somewhere during our return trek across Utah and Colorado, I called home to get some more money. Without any en route work income, I was running low on funds. My mother and father were glad to hear from me and learn about how much I was enjoying my trip. Quickly and easily my father offered to wire me some money "general delivery" to a post office somewhere ahead, wherever I said. Jim and I looked at the map and reflecting on our progress picked a small town I think in Kansas or Missouri. Dad sent fifty dollars, a small amount in today's terms, but with hamburgers at less than a quarter, hotels at three dollars a night for two people, and gas under twenty cents a gallon, fifty dollars would go a long way. At the appointed town, miracle of miracles, the telegram with my money authorized was waiting at the post office. Identify self, sign, and get paid fifty dollars, easy as that. It took less than five minutes and my easy vacation continued.

We proceeded to New York City where Jim lived. After a New York City party time with Jim's family, we drove to Lowell for a wonderful welcome home dinner with my family. We spent the night regaling my parents with our adventures from Boston to San Francisco, to Los Angeles and Hollywood, and back to Boston. The next morning, after Jimmy Grey and I had slept late, we had a hearty breakfast prepared by my mother and met the day as honorable high school graduates with fall education plans fixed and the summer deservedly off. Jimmy soon was off to see his girlfriend and make his way back to New York, and well I was not thinking of anything until my mother calmly but pointedly asked, "What are your plans to pay your father back for the money he sent you?" The question struck me like a thunderbolt, and I could only mumble something to the effect that I'd pay him back somehow. What I said did not matter to her. She followed with the comment, "Your father may have a job for you at the mill." I nodded and that was all that was said until my father came home for dinner that night.

When he arrived he was relaxed, happy, and all smiles for me. I could do no wrong it seemed and the repayment of the loan was never mentioned. My mother had obviously called him to report that I had agreed to work at the mill and he was jubilant and proud as a result. While I was ultimately free to work at anything anywhere and the mill was only an option in my father's eyes, a choice to try, to accept or move on from, for now it was a time he had dreamed about from the day I was born. When would his son join him at the mill and even someday succeed him? But the future did not matter. Now only today and tomorrow mattered and his son was ready to start mill work tomorrow.

At dinner, my father said there was a job in the supply department. It had already been arranged of course, and I would start tomorrow. I was to check in with Tom Kenny, plant superintendent, who would be expecting me at 8:00 or 8:30 a.m. in the morning. That was it. My father wished me well and soon went to bed.

The next morning my mother was up bright and early preparing a proper breakfast for a working man, and afterward I walked the mile down East Merrimack Street dressed in old working clothes ready to start work. I followed the route of my father who had left an hour earlier.

Tom Kenny met me, took me to the supply department, introduced me to Madeleine and George, and left. Somewhere along the way I signed some forms so I would get paid, $.99 per hour I think it was.

Madeleine ran the supply department and George was her first assistant. She worked the first shift, and her husband the second. She got up early, prepared breakfast for her children and a grandmother, and left for the first shift starting around 6:30 a.m. This shift schedule ended at 2:30 p.m., allowing her to get home before her children came home from school. The grandmother got the kids up and out of the house in time for school and did laundry and housework. The father slept until noon or so, then got up, ate lunch, and left for the second shift which went from around 2:30 or 3:00 p.m. to 11:00 p.m. or so in the evening. This was the pattern of many working-class families in Lowell, working split shifts so the home front and childrearing were covered. The Boott Mills employed many families with two, four, or even six members all working various shifts in various departments. Fathers, mothers, daughters, sons, brothers, sisters, uncles, aunts, cousins, huge extended families worked at the Boott Mills.

Somewhere around 10:30 or 11:00 a.m., Tom Kenny returned to tell me there was a glitch. I couldn't work without working papers said Miss Gilman, and he, red-faced about it, had to terminate my work then and there because it was against the law for me to work without working papers. He told me to go home, get a copy of my birth certificate, go back downtown to city hall, get the working papers, and return the next morning ready to work. That is exactly what I did. Glitch solved. This was my first encounter with a phenomenal employee of the Boott Mills named Miss Jennie Gilman. Miss Gilman was a very prominent member of management at the Boott Mills, but it would take me some time to experience just how much power she wielded over everyone, except for the three Flathers at the top, my grandfather, my uncle, and my father. However, even over them, she exercised a lot of influence.

As I left early for the day to get my working papers, my fellow workers all laughed at Tom Kenny's expense behind his back. No one liked to be told they had goofed, but at the Boott Mills being corrected by Miss Gilman was the worst of situations to be in, humiliation from on high!

The next day, working papers in hand, I fell into a routine quickly with George, a tall, thin, serious man, aged sixty-five or older, who was my co-worker, friend, confidante, teacher and I suppose, my watchdog. He was no Falstaff, but his job was to do his regular work while watching out for the boss's son, assuring a safe, productive, and satisfying summer work experience before I entered Harvard in the fall. I worked two months that summer and work I did each day everyday, first shift, five and a half days a week at $.99 an hour.

The supply department was the source of all spare parts for the machinery in the mill. Cams, gears, levers, switches, endless supplies of metal/wood/leather/fabric parts and components were stored away in bins from floor to ceiling. If you visit the Boott Mills today, the supply department is on the left side just beyond the car bridge over the canal, opposite where the national park staff admits visitors to the Boott Mills Museum.

Loom fixers mostly would come by and submit a requisition for various parts which we would get for them from the bins and deliver to the counter. It was like visiting an auto parts store. Also that summer, since the supply work tended to come first thing in the morning and then taper off, I had opportunities to do other things.

Tom Kenny was always hovering around making sure no one was idle. He had a host of maintenance projects that needed doing, and he was ready to launch one at the drop of a hat, whenever workers had time on their hands, and this certainly included at least some of us in the supply department. Tom was very good at this as well he had to be. The Flathers did not tolerate idleness. That summer, I poured roofing tar and repaired patches on the roof in the hot sun, loaded old textile metal junk into junk-dealer George Breasth's truck, cleaned and swept areas that had been rehabilitated for new use after a construction crew had left and before occupancy, and unloaded delivery trucks bringing in parts and supplies like soap and toilet paper. George Breasth offered to hire me at considerably more money on the spot to "crack up metal always in the hot sun," before he sold it for melt-down, and he added, "you'll be in better shape for football." My father did not think much at all of the idea of my working for anyone else and the subject was dropped. And the Boott Mills was not going to match the higher job offer, either!

Some days, especially in the afternoon, George would say "Let's take a walk," and Madeleine would nod in agreement. We would then tour the factory just like my father used to do, and George would talk and teach me as we went.

The mill was a friendly place, and George was well known and liked. People said hello and we stopped and talked with everyone. It did not take long for the word to spread in the mill that George was working with the boss's son. I did not deny being the boss's son. In fact I recall full acceptance and understanding of my role. But I tried to downplay it and be a regular guy. I think I was successful because confidences were shared with me that wouldn't have been if I hadn't been trusted.

The supply department had a hot plate to heat coffee water and this was heavily used on arrival in the morning and at mid-morning, lunch, and early afternoon. It was illegal per mill rule so it had to be hidden and operated surreptitiously. There was always a lookout stationed at the front counter to keep watch for supervisors or even more problematic, a Flather coming by. When Tom Kenny was sighted, the hot plate would go out and we would jump to hide the pot as well as the incriminating evidence of coffee cup rings and crumbs. We wouldn't be evidencing productivity if we were caught drinking coffee or snacking.

When my father came by the supply department, his presence had the same effect as Tom Kenny's. When my uncle Frederick appeared there, it was tense. He did not come by often, but when he did he was serious and formal, while still friendly. The truth was I did not know my uncle well at all because I saw him just one day a year at Thanksgiving, and that was little more than saying hello, but of course the workers did not know this. They would assume an uncle is an uncle. In the early days, both my father and Uncle Frederick made periodic appearances, but after a while, thank heaven, they remained in the front office. The best thing about Frederick's visits was that they were brief. Frederick came by because he felt he should see his nephew, but more on this later. Over time, neither my father nor my uncle checked on me. For my part, I was happy to be left alone to make my own way.

Madeleine, the department boss, but also the only woman of the group, mothered us all. She often brought in coffee cakes, cookies and pies, all baked at home. There was always a stream of chatter and mill gossip, and she was always at the center. This happened all the time. The happiest of times were when we were sitting around, talking and snacking all on company time, while also filling supply orders if there was a call to do so. Sometimes, she looked tired, physically worn down, wan, and pale. She was thin to begin with and coughed a lot. I imagine that she was possibly anemic and physically drained by working a full factory shift while also managing her family home front. This was long before the now well-established two-income family, but blue-collar family women have always worked in greater numbers and they certainly did at the Boott Mills. Women like Madeleine were everywhere especially as spinners and weavers, in all departments except the machine shop, loom fixing, boiler room, dye house, and the aforementioned cotton bale opening room. The front office secretaries, dressed to the nines, were younger and probably more transient, en route to marriage and leaving the work force, for a while at least. Among the production workers, women seemed to stay on with continuity. The textile mills in Lowell by my time in the 1950's were on their last legs. Young people were not seeking work there, whether male or female. Service jobs in cleaner surroundings were more attractive to people of my generation. The number of workers I saw who were in their twenties was never more than a handful; less than five out of six hundred people perhaps. Then again, textile mills in Lowell were not hiring since business was slowing. The first mill that closed up shop did so in 1923, the same year my father and my uncle started their careers at the Boott. The mill business was going south or moving to Puerto Rico. Five mills had left Lowell by 1930 and just about all the others were gone by the 1960's. Ultimately the industry would go overseas, mostly to developing nations. Today all one has to do is read labels to see how diversified the source of our clothing has become. Surely, for a young person, this was no career path to start on. Thus my father's entire career was accompanied by a relentlessly shrinking New England textile industry.

During this period, Lowell was perpetually near the top of the list of communities in the United States with the highest chronic unemployment figures. Lowell's unemployment was twenty-five percent and this went on year after year, despite the successors to the textile industry, such as Raytheon, Textron,

CBS Wytron, and General Electric, often using portions of the same old buildings.

Lowell's population in the 1920's was over 130,000. In the 1950's it was in the 90,000-100,000 range where it still is today, more or less. This is despite the large immigration of people from Southeast Asia, principally from Cambodia but also from Latin America and Central America.

During my tours with George, I remember that at the end of each industrial building was a mill tower with stairs and each step was covered with a metal plate that said "Boott Cotton Mills." These stair towers were unheated and in winter they were cold. I had to be careful to slow down on these stairs because George would start to breathe deeply, and I wondered if he had a health problem or if he felt he had to keep up with the boss's son. I feared for his safety and so would take rests myself. If you look at those towers, all six floors of them, almost anyone would want to take a rest once or twice along the way to the top floor. Afterwards we would walk the mill as my father and I had done years before, talking to workers and again learning how to tie a weaver's knot, how a loom operates, what the intricacies are in the spinning rooms, and similar textile technology issues.

I especially enjoyed visiting the dye house and would have liked to work there. The dye house was on the ground floor and consisted of two cement pits full of whatever brightly-colored dye was being used that day. At each end was a roll of bleached cloth on a roller that would be unwound through the dye bath to a take-up roller at the other end. The process would go back and forth until the dye color was considered acceptable to a standard. Then another roll of cloth would be dyed.

There were just a handful of male workers there and they wore rubber overalls with boots attached. It was hot and they always seemed to be sweating profusely. Since peroxide was used in the process, they had white streaks in their hair. I wanted some of those white streaks, but it was not to be.

I also liked to visit the boiler room where steam-generated electricity was produced. Here, two men shoveled coal into the furnace. One of them was African- American, the only person of color I ever saw in the mill. Historically, the textile industry was not a place African- Americans worked in or were welcome in, and throughout the nineteenth and twentieth centuries, the number of African- Americans living in Lowell was small. I did not have African-American classmates in school until I was at Harvard and even there the number was small.

13. First Payday.

At the end of the first pay period, I eagerly awaited my first paycheck. Checks were distributed by hand. On payday the supervisors went to the front office, the payroll department, picked up the batch of checks for their area and distributed them one by one.

On this day, George, Madeleine and the others each received a check from Tom Kenny. Each one looked at the amount with a private glance and pocketed the check. There might be a comment or a question in hushed tones between workers, but that was the weekly ritual. On my first payday there was no check for me. Tom Kenny seemed a little embarrassed. I recall feeling funny when he told me that my check was ready but had to be picked up by me in person. He wasn't about to explain why or add anything to this. He said I was to go see Miss Gilman in the front office and only Miss Gilman could get it. My fellow workers rolled their eyes as they glanced at each other knowingly and with sympathy for me. I must have looked disappointed and frustrated as they allowed me to go right away. It wouldn't be right to be without a check for one moment longer and my getting paid now was more important than any work that had to be done by the supply group. They would cover for me.

So I walked the short way across the roadway below the bridge over the canal to the front office where Miss Gilman held court. Every company needs an employee like Miss Gilman, at least the Boott Mills did or at least the Flather family managers did. She was a serious person who never seemed to smile. Everyone lowered their voice when talking about her as if she might overhear them, although she was yards and yards away in a totally different part of the mill. No one said anything ill of her, but the body language was all that it took for one to surmise how formidable this person was. When Miss Gilman was the subject everyone walked on eggshells. I even think the Flathers walked on eggshells, on occasion, with her. In retrospect, she was extremely valuable to them. She was honest, trustworthy, loyal and hard working. I believe that every company needs a Miss Gilman; at least every family-run company like the Boott Mills.

I found the following pages in the Boott Mills files now housed in the Lowell Center for History, with the title," How to Succeed." The author is unstated, but it applies to office workers and could well have been written by Miss Gilman, who supervised office workers. It sounds like her and I think she was the author. It also echoes my father's values so he could have written it or had input as well. He always exhorted us to work hard and be as invaluable to our boss as possible, so that when the boss got promoted, he or she would take us along. This is clearly the theme of "How to Succeed."

HOW TO SUCCEED

Do not talk in the office unless it is necessary. The office is not the place in which to visit. Learn to answer the telephone, but do not use it more than is necessary. Discourage your friends from calling you to the telephone simply for social purposes, or from calling you at your place of business. Remember that when you go into an office you assume the responsibility of doing the business placed in your hands correctly and to the best of your ability. Therefore, take pains. Be accurate and neat in your work. Do everything a little better than you are expected to. Be cheerful and obliging when asked to do work outside of your line. Try and fill in your leisure moments in a way that will help your employer. Study his work in all its details, so that you will know how to aid him. Make yourself necessary to him. Everyone has peculiarities; learn what are your employer's and adapt yourself to them. Above all, be pleasant or no one will want you around. Be punctual. Do a little more work than you are paid for rather than less. Be trustworthy. Do not talk of your employer's affairs even to your best friend. Let him feel that he can trust you with the minutest details of his business, and that no one will be the wiser for it.

> Proceed in this way, and you will not only win the respect of everyone who comes into the office, but you will become so valuable to your employer that he will prize you as he does his right hand, and thus you will earn and gain promotion.

I had grown up in the shadow of Miss Gilman. She was the only person in the mill with whom I had any kind of acquaintance before being employed there. Yes I had met Tom

Kenny and others, casually, during my boyhood tours with my father. But my generation, my siblings, we all knew Miss Gilman.

She used to arrive in December with a birthday present for my oldest sister Kitsey, for Kitsey's birthday on December 19 fell just before the holidays. Kitsey, being the first born, was the special focus of Miss Gilman's attention and generosity. Miss Gilman would arrive in a car driven by someone else who kept the engine running. She would ring the bell, ask for Kitsey, and wait to deliver the gift in person. She would not enter. Kitsey for her part was expected to behave politely, thank Miss Gilman profusely, and act as though Miss Gilman had made her day. They had lots to talk about by the open door because Miss Gilman never came in for fear she'd upset the family routine. She hadn't been invited and besides, despite her vaunted, powerful, and respected position at the mill, she was still just an employee of the mill. Even special employees of the Flathers had their place, especially in the management family.

Well Kitsey hated it. She would happily have forgiven the gift and devolved the accolade on another sibling, but she could not. This could not be; she was the one and only, the first born, and no one else would ever get a gift. The gift was Miss Gilman's way of acknowledging her special relationship with Rogers and ingratiating herself with him and his "wonderful wife Betty," which is how she referred to my mother.

Miss Gilman on the surface was austere, superior, and brutally efficient. Behind this exterior I'm sure she was kind and wished to be with me at the mill and with Kitsey at the time of the annual birthday gift, but her personality was controlling. In private, Kitsey reacted and bellowed and complained, but was forced to do her parents' bidding and she always did so, well and faithfully, albeit with a not so quiet acceptance. We siblings, knowing of Kitsey's pain and discomfort, reveled in Miss Gilman's visits. We looked out the windows, hooted and hollered and urged Kitsey on, increasing her pain and discomfort. Of course that's what you do to siblings. Finally, My mother would have to step in and give Kitsey some loving attention. This was all a foreshadowing my own relationship with Miss Gilman. The boss's son had to learn as his sister had done over the years, to be gracious, polite and friendly. If he was ever to be successful in his own right as a worker and as the boss's son, he had better get along with Miss Gilman. His grandfather, his uncle and his father would not hear of having it otherwise. This was the least it would take to be a successful heir apparent and nothing less would be tolerated.

Later I learned that Miss Gilman had a powerful position in the mill and a special relationship with the Flather family as the only person who knew where all the money was and how it was spent because she handled the management payroll. In other words, the Flathers decided themselves, subject to the board of directors, what each worker was going to be paid. Basically my grandfather decided this but Miss Gilman carried out these payroll decisions for the top management. She made other personnel decisions as well. She ran the payroll department for the supervisors including Tom Kenny. You better believe Miss Gilman had power and everyone in the mill gave her respect, deference, and space.

So, I arrived at her office. I had been doing a lot of physical labor that day. I think it had been a tar day on the roof and I looked the part: dirty, sweaty, and smelly with plenty of evidence that I had been in tar. In the room were three or four neat rows of small typing desks perhaps fifteen of them, each occupied by a youngish, well-dressed woman sitting straight as an arrow, typing away. Those were the days of many carbons and skill levels for typing with carbons were exacting. Miss Gilman's desk was at the front on a raised platform and she supervised, staring down at all below. As I entered, the women kept typing with nary a side glance at me but I am sure they observed me closely.

I walked up to the front of the room and Miss Gilman greeted me in a loud, slow voice so all present could hear. "John Rogers Flather, Junior" emphasizing each word, "how wonderful it is to see you. How wonderful it is to have another Flather in the Boott Mills. Are you enjoying your work here?" I replied "Yes" and could have died.

The next few minutes were a mirage. She asked questions and I mumbled answers. I don't remember much of what was talked about. I felt humiliated, stressed and dazed. Finally she opened her top desk drawer, found my check conveniently placed there, and handed it to me. I thanked her and beat a hasty retreat. Back in the supply department everyone was grinning and laughing at my expense, not going too far but asking me how my friend Miss Gilman was and had I made it with Miss Gilman and had I enjoyed my visit with Miss Gilman. I felt that I had a problem but hadn't figured out what to do about it. This special payroll procedure had to change! It could not become the routine, but how or what to do?

The next payday when Tom Kenny came around again,

everyone else got their check and looked at me in anticipation of what would happen next. Once again he said Miss Gilman had my check and I should go and get it from her. My co-workers watched me intently. I really felt angry, and I didn't give a damn who the supervisor was or what the repercussions might be. I was not going to go to that woman to get my paycheck that day or any day, ever. In as polite a voice as I could muster, I told Tom Kenny that I was not going to Miss Gilman's office to get my paycheck. I wanted to have my check given to me each payday just like everyone else, no more and no less. That altercation over, everyone quickly seemed to find something productive to do and they disappeared. I was left there alone as Tom Kenny turned and left without further discussion.

Some minutes passed before Tom Kenny returned and smiling broadly but saying absolutely nothing, handed me my check. I thanked him and he said, "You're welcome," and left again. There was no explanation. The word Gilman was never mentioned, but everyone else enjoyed the situation to the hilt. They weren't laughing this time, but cheering, not loudly or excessively, but cheering it was. They seemed to get pleasure from Miss Gilman's stepping down even if it was only on account of the boss's son. And I think they were enjoying some of Tom Kenny's discomfort too because he was their immediate boss.

In addition to dealing with Tom Kenny and Miss Gilman, I also had to deal with the real bosses, my father and Frederick Flather, Junior, my uncle Frederick. Behind their backs, the workers referred to them respectively as Frederick and Rogers. When my uncle came by, I would tense up because as stated previously, I did not know him well at all. I believed he could be demanding and strict but I did not know that from firsthand experience. Now I feel that my uncle was genuinely interested in my working at the mill and was sincere in his occasional visits. That first summer he came by perhaps once every week or two. Later, when I worked at the mill during summers and vacations, he did not come by at all. The novelty had worn off and there was no longer any need to do so.

My father also came by, but in similar fashion he also began to leave me alone as time went by. He came perhaps once a week at the beginning, but in later work stints he never came at all. I liked that and it showed that I had settled into a routine and my presence could be taken for granted by everyone.

After my last work stint in the mill in the spring of 1954, the mill having ceased production later that year and I had graduated from college, married Becky, and moved to Pensacola, Florida to commence naval flight training, Uncle Frederick and Aunt Edith called us one day wishing to come and pay a visit to our rented bungalow home. They were on a motoring trip through the south and were passing through Pensacola on their way to Mobile, Alabama and then to Louisiana. Becky and I rushed to clean the house and within moments they were on our doorstep. We served them tea and cookies. The Boott Mills was hardly mentioned but they did talk about where they had traveled thus far and were they were heading to next. Becky and I enjoyed telling them about our navy life and my flight-training program.

They stayed for about an hour and then were on their way. At the time, I was surprised by their visit. They were reaching out despite a pattern of family suspicion and paranoia, with seemingly little or no incentive to do so. Looking back, I am grateful for their kind gesture that day. Their warm and friendly manner had spanned a family divide in a special and poignant way.

14. Work in Other Departments.

During Christmas vacation of 1950, I worked in the bleachery where an endless "rope" of toweling was run through a bleach wash, left to remain damp in a huge wood storage box for a while and then dried on a series of rotating metal drums with hot steam pumped inside. As the toweling emerged from the bleach bath, you could grab the rope of toweling loosely as it traveled past and get a super hand wash. You were left with the bleach smell on your hands but two hands were never cleaner!

I spent several vacations during the spring and fall of 1951 and '52 rebuilding old looms into faster, more productive and efficient ones. The older looms had been used for weaving grey (unfinished) goods. This was what corduroy was called before the ridges were cut and brushed together to produce its special feel and shape. The economics of textiles were becoming increasing demanding on northern mills, such that the Boott Mills found it more profitable (or less costly) to buy grey goods from southern mills and ship them north for finishing (cutting, brushing, dying and packaging). It was clear that the end of making and selling corduroy from Lowell was at hand. All that the Boott Mills was hanging onto then was its ability to finish goods expertly which southern mills could surely do as well in time. The Boott Mills was selling via its established distribution channels to satisfied customers and had a reputation for delivering a quality product intact. Since price was everything, these advantages were not really advantages and would soon be illusory.

I remember when corduroy became very popular after World War II. In the 1930's, towels and curtains were the Boott's main business. Whenever my father and I went into a washroom (this was before the time when paper towels replaced cloth towels in public washrooms), he would always check to see if the towels contained the Boott trademark label. He did the same in hotel rooms with the curtains. As often as not, we found Boott Mills labels.

With World War II, production was turned over to military uniforms, so-called twill, with towels and curtains relegated to little or no production at all.

After World War II, the curtain market collapsed. Americans turned to buying ready-made curtains which were produced by other firms more cheaply or custom dictated not hanging curtains at all. Paper towels began to replace cloth towels in public washrooms.

Thus, after World War II, the Boott Mills still had a toweling business and increased production of corduroy to make up for the demise of the curtain market, but soon the toweling market was at stake as well.

While the Boott Mills pioneered some quality improvements in corduroy, e.g. softer versions, it was always a tough market. By this time every market was a tough market. For most northern textile mills corduroy had historically been a school material for children. Try as they might, it was an uphill climb to increase sales of corduroy year round by convincing the public it was a year round fabric that could be worn by men and women as well as children, and could also be worn to the office. The stereotype of corduroy then as a material for school use for children only in the fall constituted a stubborn challenge to improvement and broadening in the market place.

I always found the corduroy process interesting. The cloth was cut by circular metal knives hung on a bar with a knife set to cut each round edge in half without cutting through the cloth to make any tears. The tolerances were very close since the knife had to cut only the top of the cloth. At that point the cut cloth would be brushed by a two-way brush whereby the cut ends on one side of the cut seam would be brushed together with the cut ends on the adjoining cut seam and so on across the cloth. At that point corduroy could be brushed by the hand either way and the appearance was the same. Style and convention dictated, however, that corduroy only go one way so that a hand motion in one direction would produce a smooth surface and in the opposite direction a darker, rougher surface. This effect was achieved by a final one-way brushing.

The Boott Mills made its own brushing machines, both two-way and one-way brushing machines, in the machine shop. Large metal frames were welded together on which were hung brushes on belts or arms that went back and forth at high speed with an electric motor installed below. These machines made in Lowell were presumably cheaper and more effective than what could be purchased. I suspect my uncle Frederick, an engineer, had a major hand in such mechanical developments because this was an area he was interested in and used his technical abilities to their fullest extent.

It was in 1953 that I recall first seeing grey goods coming in from the south. Initially there were quality control problems. Workers inspecting the material were finding blemishes. A special area for inspection was set up with long tables installed in a small room cleared of machinery. The rolls of material were unrolled and inspected and blemishes marked and cut out. Reports were prepared for communicating to the southern mill that had produced the material and for issuance of credits. The quality control produced quality improvements so it wasn't long before the quality of the southern product was comparable to that which could be made in the north. The idea of buying grey goods from the south more cheaply than they could be made in the north became the only profitable way to go. This practice followed management's failed attempt to get the union (TWUA/CIO) to increase productivity and cut costs.

In a January 27, 1954 letter to the union, management wrote in part, "Rejected work load proposal. Unable to continue grey goods manufacturing. Discontinuing card, spinning, and weaving." In effect, the Boott Mills ceased to be in the cotton textiles manufacturing business. Making cloth from a bale of cotton had been the heart and soul of the mill since 1835, and this work and all the workers involved were now irrelevant to its future.

In the meantime, the inspectors complained that Boott-produced grey goods never had these blemishes. They must have known that sooner or later their jobs would be transferred too, just like the grey goods production workers had experienced. They did not like to talk very much about working on someone else's grey goods. It was almost like they were scabs who needed to do this work in secret.

15. Loom Fixing -- The Best Job Ever.

After my two stints in the bleachery, the following week I was assigned to work with a group of machinists who were cutting down the large grey goods corduroy looms to half size. The rebuilt looms were twice as fast and would increase the productivity of the toweling manufacturing process markedly. The width of the towel product was probably in the range of twenty-two to thirty-two inches as opposed to the sixty-eight to seventy-two inches of corduroy cloth. Thus if one used the wider corduroy looms for making much narrower toweling, the shuttle would travel almost twice as far each pass thereby slowing down the volume of production.

The newer rebuilt looms were marvelous little gems to behold. They were like new, small and easy to service, and you could reach any part from one standing place, but what recommended them most was their speed. Using the same cam shuttle throwing levers and harnesses, the shuttle flew at greater speed across half the distance and back again. I don't recall the exact increases, but for talking purposes let's just say that the rebuilt towel looms could operate at double the productivity of the corduroy looms since the shuttle carried its thread back and forth less than half the distance of the original loom before renovation.

We would cut the frame roughly into thirds, remove the middle and weld the two ends back together. Then with new and reconditioned parts, the loom would be reassembled from the floor up and moved to a production floor. I learned to skin my knuckles with a wrench, to overtighten the nuts and skim the threads off of the bolts, and I can still hear the quiet and patient pronouncements from a senior co-worker, "Easy, Roger, easy, just turn it this far and no more." After a while I kind of got it. I really enjoyed this work. We were alone in an otherwise empty weaving room full of dust and dim light where the large looms were no longer in use. There were about three or four men including me. The numbers would vary. From time to time, a loom fixer or machinist would be dispatched to help. Sometimes Tom Kenny himself came by, and as he was dressed as a supervisor, he would roll up his sleeves, tuck in his necktie, and go to work carefully so as not to ruin his clothes. He probably hadn't done work like this for years, but he seemed to enjoy being a member of the crew and I certainly enjoyed working with him. There was a lot of talk. He probably did this kind of work years ago before he deservedly moved up to become plant superintendent. He smiled as he helped assemble the rebuilt looms, I think both from the pleasure of still having the old skill of tools in hand and the right feel, and also to prove to the rest of us that he was truly just as good at his work now as when he did it for a living years ago, and certainly just as good if not better than any of us. I enjoyed him; the old master cannot be beat!

The time flew. In addition to the work and the collegiality, I enjoyed seeing the looms emerge off the floor from a pile of frames and parts. The electric motor was attached last and then, under the close attention of a loom fixer, the loom would be started. The fixer would look, feel, touch, and listen. He would hear the mistakes as well as feel and see them. Shut down, adjust, restart, adjust, instruct one of us to do something, adjust, restart, trouble shoot, that was the process and one nifty little loom was ready to make some toweling and make money for everyone for a few years more. If there was more than one fixer on hand, such as when Tom Kenny was there, there would be discussion indeed debate on which adjustments needed to be made. I was all ears. It was quite a production, really a seminar, with the best experts anywhere in the world at work, and they seemed intent on outperforming each other.

16. The Incredible Jake.

The next vacation work assignment was one of my happiest. I was told to wait in the supply department for Jake, a loom fixer with whom I was to apprentice. While waiting, I caught up with Madeleine and George, a happy first day back for me.

An hour or so into the day a stocky, muscular, blonde man appeared carrying his toolbox. With a big smile and lots of friendly talk, he joked around with the workers, grabbed a cup of illicit coffee and sampled some of Madeleine's Danish. He accused them of doing nothing but drinking coffee all day and said that he was going to tell on them. He then greeted me warmly.

In due course we set out across the mill yard with me carrying an armful of heavy replacement parts and his toolbox. I wondered how he managed without me to carry his parts. In any case, we went up the stairs through long rooms most of them empty of production workers, some in operation, waved to workers and finally came to our station. There a weaver asked Jake what took him so long, but just in humor. She lost money when a loom was down and his absence seemed much longer to her than it should have been. I silently agreed, recalling the coffee, Danish, gossip, and sitting around we had done back in the office. We went to work and soon had her loom up and running and producing cloth for the mill and money for her pocket.

We next went to do a tie-in. This was done when the warp of threads came to an end and a new warp was sent on a low, wheeled cart to replace the empty warp. The warp was very heavy. We would remove the old warp and install the new one. If done right the loom would shut down before it ran the warp empty such that with a special tie-in machine all the threads of the nearly depleted warp were tied automatically to the threads of the new warp. This would otherwise have been a huge job with hundreds of individual threads to be tied and then threaded through the threadles, harnesses, etc. That's the way it was done for years before the tie-in machine was invented. The tie-in machine was small and mobile, and at the Boott Mills it was mostly operated by women.

We also worked on the auto shut-off controls. Before these were added years ago, a loom could run on indefinitely, if no one was watching carefully, with a broken thread or a bobbin out of thread, serving to ruin that piece of cloth. A broken thread creates an empty space in the cloth, a blemish. Also if the bobbin thread broke or if the bobbin ran out and a new one was not installed, the empty shuttle would continue to go back and forth uselessly since no cloth would be woven. Meanwhile the take-up roll would continue to collect the warp threads and without the bobbin thread there would be a long swathe of unwoven warp rolled over the earlier woven cloth, not good.

The auto shut-offs prevented these problems from occurring and improved productivity, quality, and pay for the weavers.

Sometimes the auto shut-offs broke and the loom fixer would have to repair or replace them.

We also did a lot of adjusting, especially to the harness and levers that threw the shuttle. These were cam operated and when the bump on the cam wheel came around and raised the lever and transferred that motion to the throwing arm, great force was produced and the shuttle with bobbin thread inside flew across. There was danger if the adjustments were not well done and within accepted tolerances. The timing of the shuttle-throwing actions had to be perfectly and precisely set. I heard stories over and over of a shuttle shooting up and out of the loom and across the room. If it hit someone in the head in full flight it could kill them or certainly injure them. The shuttle, about fifteen inches long and made of wood, had sharp metal sheeting on each end honed to a sharp point. It looked like an artillery projectile.

I cannot say that I had the natural feel for being a good machinist. I don't think I have the manual dexterity or perhaps the mental focus to stay on task with machinery the way people who work on machines happily and successfully do. My grandfather was a machinist and had a toolbox. Somehow this inheritance did not make it to my generation. When we five kids were learning to drive cars, we bemoaned our mechanical ignorance. Anyway, I enjoyed my days with Jake and became good at repetitive machine work once I got the hang of it.

One day I came in and Jake was not smiling or talking. He looked tired and beat and who was I to question him about anything? I always took great pains to be cheerful, to work hard and to "go with the flow". As the boss' son I had to get along. It was that simple.

As Jake ordered some parts, I was quiet. He ordered a lot more than usual. I wondered how I would carry them all, the heavy cams, etc. Then he said, "Let's go. We've got a ton of work to do" and waved goodbye to the supply department staff. He behaved as if he was doing the most important job in the mill that day, certainly more important than anything they were likely to do. Usually Jake told Madeleine where he would be in case anyone was looking for him but today when she asked, he was vague. Loom fixers were always in demand and in short supply. The weavers complained that there were not enough fixers. I wondered if the mill had cut back too much on fixers, to save money. The weavers probably had a point. In due course, I picked up all the parts and put them in a burlap bag. Then I obediently followed Jake out. He was carrying almost nothing.

Silently we walked across the lower mill yard, up the stairs of a tower, then through loom room after loom room, past all of the rooms where workers were still weaving, then through a couple of old empty dusty rooms where silent rows of unused looms met the eye, and finally to the last building, the top floor, beyond any place I had been for work. It was another weaving room closed to production. What in heaven's name was our job today? No one had talked about this room coming back on line, and it would be unlikely to come back on line anyway because it was so far removed from all the production processes that would lead up to it and lead inventory to it. Yet here I was huffing and puffing behind Jake with an extra supply of heavy replacement parts. It did not figure.

It was a beautiful winter day. The room was unheated and cold, but he stopped where the sun was brilliantly shining in from the two sides of a far corner, creating a swathe of warmth in one place. This is where he put his toolbox down. He then scrounged around and located a piece of linoleum or canvas (often placed under a loom to catch oil drippings), spread it out on the floor under the loom that was receiving the most sun, crawled underneath, put his arm under his head and let out a huge groan.

I was still standing there holding the parts when Jake exclaimed "Don't just stand there. Get down for Christ's sake! Get down! We don't want anyone to see us. Pull that piece of canvas up over there and lie on it." So I did what he told me to do.

Then he proceeded to say, "Jesus what a night! Jesus what a woman! I was in this bar for only one beer and then I wanted to go to bed because I was tired but she came over to me. We had a beer and then another and another. I don't know how many. We were so drunk. Then she invited me back to her place and she flirted all over me, Jesus what a body! I never experienced anything like it. We made love, then we fell asleep and in the middle of the night she woke up and we made love a second time, but I was dead and I could hardly do it. We fell asleep until about two hours ago and then she wanted to do it a third time. I got through it, but God, am I exhausted. "I can't work. I got no sleep. I'm hung over. Dangerous to work when you are this way. I've got to rest. I don't care what you do but stay down so anyone coming into the room can't see us and stay quiet. And never work on machinery when you're out of it."

So what was I to do? I had been on a schedule of work from 6:30 a.m. to 2:30 p.m., meaning that I was up at 5:00 a.m. and out of the house by 6:00 a.m. Then after work I would rush home, shower and drive to see Becky. We would go out for a hamburger and take in a movie. I should have been home in bed by 10:30 p.m. but in fact I was getting home by 12:00 a.m. or later. I was tired too. Happily I slept. There we were, the two of us, secretly asleep on the floor under a loom in a beautiful sunlit corner. We must have been there about three hours or so when finally I woke up, but I had to stay quiet while Jake continued to snore on.

When he got up he looked at me and said, "Well, I guess we'd better find a use for some of these parts, and what we don't use today we'll stash and use tomorrow."

I asked him why we brought so many parts. We could never use all these parts in one day of fixing unless there was something I didn't know. I could easily figure out by now how much time it took to do a repair job using each part. The usual process was to take out the old part, install the new one, adjust, test, adjust, and move on. You could do just so many of these jobs a day. He looked at me like I was stupid to not have figured it out.

Finally he said, "I needed them back in supply to see me take all these parts, even extra parts, so they would know I had a full day's schedule and couldn't get to anyone's emergency request for fixing." When a machine broke down, the weavers would send a message to the supply department to get the fixer up there fast so they would not lose the money they expected to earn. The supply department knew where the fixer was that day because he would tell Madeleine, "I'll be in 6-2 or I'll be in 4-3 and after that I'll be back here later this a.m." Thus the supply department would be able to give the harried weaving room an estimate on where Jake was and when he might show.

On this day, however, he did not let them know where he was setting out to work or when he might return. The extra parts that I was carrying so laboriously and his air of confidence and authority were premised on giving an impression of an extra busy work day so they didn't try to reach him or suggest that anyone else try to reach him.

By late morning we returned to an operating area and did a couple of easy fixes, none involving electricity. Then we stashed the extra parts I was still carrying around, took lunch, washed up, and finished for the day. I was so well rested that I could go on a longer date with Becky that night with no pain. But what I really treasured that day was the trust Jake had shown in me, the boss' son, to philander so overtly because he was hung over so badly, with nary a caution or a worry. He said absolutely nothing to me about any concern he might have had about my talking to anyone. Of course I suppose it helped too that I dozed off with him. Now if everyone did this what would happen to the textile mill? Jake was truly unforgettable.

The Boott Mills with the Merrimack River in the foreground

MY dad WOrkS in the BOOTT Mill.
He Goes around and Sees than Things are
being made right, sometimes, he goes To
NEW York and Phil 7 delphia to see if
HErn Sell towells and curtains.
This is what is done in the Mill.
1. BUY cotton
2 Spin ino Yarn
3 Weave into cloth
4 Bleach and dye
5 CUT, Sew into curtains
    and towels
6 Sell

My school report: What Does Your Father Do At Work? Page 1 (1940)

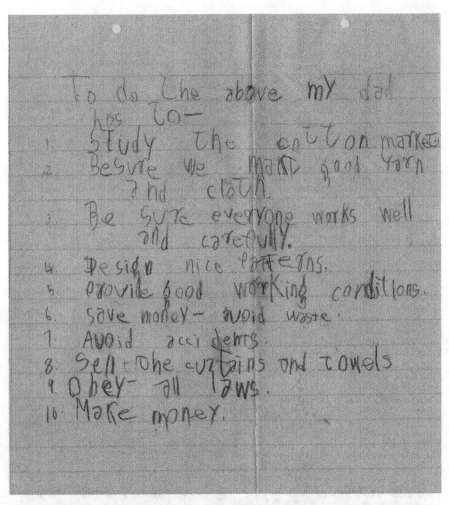

To do the above my dad has to—
1. Study the cotton market
2. Besure we make good yarn and cloth.
3. Be sure everyone works well and carefully.
4. Design nice patterns.
5. Provide good working conditions.
6. Save money— avoid waste.
7. Avoid accidents.
8. Sell the curtains and towels
9. Obey— all laws.
10. Make money.

My school report: What Does Your Father Do At Work? Page 2 (1940)

Pile of coal in the Boott Mills parking lot during World War II

Army Navy E flag flying over the Boott Mills during World War II

Girl looking out of a 2nd story window during the
Army Navy E Ceremony (possibly Kitsey)

Grandfather about to give a speech during the Army Navy E Ceremony

Army Navy E Ceremony: from left to right: John R. Flather, Frederick A. Flather, two U.S. Military officers and Frederick Flather, Jr.

Frederick Arthur Flather, "Grandfather", 1867-1967.

Portrait painting of John Rogers and Frederick, Jr. as children (artist not known)

John Rogers Flather, March 6, 1899 –1979.
Year photo taken: 1923. Age: 24 years.

Frederick A. Flather, Jr. March 6, 1900 – 1986.   Year
photo taken: 1923. Age: 23 years.

John R. Flather, Jr., 1933 – 2004.
Year photo taken:1950. Age: 17 years.

"The Boss" and his son
Thanksgiving Day, 1978
(Newell and Kate's dining room)

17. Quality-Control Lab and the Opera Too.

One of my last work assignments was in the quality-control and testing lab. The lab was isolated in a distant part of the mill and there was only one worker there, the chief quality-control analyst. In prior years there had been a full staff, but the lab was an easy place for management to cut back when cuts had to be made. I could still imagine a room full of busy test people, occupying all of the test stands, when the mill was running three shifts at full production. The lab was set up like a school science lab with several rows of test benches. Each bench top had a small material test device bolted to the top in which the two ends of a production sample were clipped viselike and the material stretched to the preset strength standard. Of course the stretching could go on until the material ripped apart, something I liked to do, much to the consternation of my supervisor, because breaking a material apart wasn't part of the lab routine.

Each day samples would arrive and we would test them and record the results in a notebook. It did not appear that anyone really cared what the results were or that anyone even looked at the notebooks. There did not seem to be anyone accessing the reports, which we just filed away. I guess if a piece of material failed a test we would have called that fact to someone's attention. To say the least this was a low-key, low-stress, almost passive operation. It was like being in a science lab in school only less so, and I was totally bored. Given that I was once again burning my candle at both ends, seeing Becky on dates several nights a week and pushing the time clock very early each morning, I was prone to falling asleep at the test table. There really wasn't enough to do and it reminded me of school which I wanted to get away from.

My co-worker was a very interesting person however. He was the only person like him that I met in the mill. He was soft spoken, quiet, unassuming, quirky, bespectacled, and serious in demeanor and intellect. In a word he was a nerd, but a very nice nerd. A bachelor, he lived alone and very simply. Everyday he would bring a lunch with him. It was like not like any other lunch I saw people in the mill bring. He would open up a large cloth napkin, set it up like a table cloth, and serve himself in style with metal utensils on a china plate. He would bring a meal, not a sandwich and a drink, but a full meal and he would eat it with deliberation, happily and with relish.

His big interest was the opera, which he would give anything to see. He would save up and plan ahead for each year's season in Boston. When the opera season opened, he was ready to buy his tickets and afforded himself two, but never more than two performances each season. I was virtually ignorant of opera and had never seen one. Here I was meant to be a sophisticated and educated Harvard type, but I knew zilch about opera and was patiently introduced to it in a textile mill by a man who had never been to college. So the work part of this assignment was something that tried my patience to the limit, but the personal relationship with Mr. Opera was one I appreciated greatly.

Nowadays, blended fabric, nylon, dacron, orlon, and other synthetic blends of woolen and cotton threads are de rigueur, but in the early '50s so recently after World War II that the rage for plastics was still unabated, such materials were still new. Some worked out and some didn't. It would take a while to perfect the blending and to determine customer preference. One example was present in the lab. In the corner was a loom set up to weave cotton and nylon threads together. The problem was that the two materials parted under different stresses producing material where the nylon threads held fast and the accompanying cotton threads broke apart.

This research had been undertaken in the lab and in this particular case the product had failed to meet the quality-control standard and had been abandoned. Thereafter the economic future of the mill was so much in question that the research and development function ceased to exist. The quality control and testing lab was one more example of a mill on its last legs, dying right before one's eyes.

18. A Real Textile Worker at Last.

The jobs that I had in the mill were essentially all in a support category. I never made cloth as such. I worked in the quality-control lab and in the supply department, and I did manual labor tarring the roof and doing other plant maintenance and clean-up chores. I moved junk and old machinery out and helped replenish, upgrade, and rebuild looms and I worked in the bleachery. Perhaps I got closest to the actual textile process when doing loom fixing and in the bleachery where the cloth was washed and made ready for dying and final cutting and packaging. But I never was a spinner or a card operator or a weaver. If the machine shop was the heart of the mill for one kind of worker, then spinning, card operation and weaving were the heart of the mill for another kind of worker. The machine shop folk were high on anyone's pedestal, but they could do their skilled mechanical work in a number of capacities in a number of industries and could move on to other jobs as need be, which is what they did when the mill was on strike and when it finally closed. The machine shop workers were all male.

On the other hand, the workers who actually made the

cloth were the people that the music of James Taylor in *Working* so aptly celebrates.

Mill Work Song

Granddad was a sailor. He blew in off the water.
My father was a farmer and I his only daughter.
I took up with a no good mill workin' man from
Massachusetts who died from too much whisky and
leaves me these three faces to feed.
Mill work ain't easy, mill work ain't hard,
Mill work ain't nothing but a God damn awful
    boring job.
But my life has been wasted and I have been the
fool to let this manufacturer use my body for a tool.
I get to ride home in the evening, staring
at my hands, swearing by my sorrow that a young
girl ought to stand a better chance.
But may I work this mill as long as I am able
And never meet the man whose name is on the
    label.
It's me and my machine for the rest of the
morning, for the rest of the afternoon gone, and
the rest of my life.

When you see Sally Field in the movie *Norma Rae* standing up on a desk holding up the strike sign she was in a production room. When Richard Gere in *An Officer and a Gentleman* goes into a mill to find Debra Winger and carry her out to a marriage with a naval aviator, she was tending a production machine in a paper mill. The heart and soul of a textile mill was where the cloth was made.

There was just one day when I felt like a real textile worker. I was in a weaving room making cloth. It was a cold, blustery, winter day and the mill was able to start up only slowly and partially because the city was under two feet of snow. The workers couldn't get there other than on foot which is how I got there, and they trickled in all morning.

It was like any winter day after the snow had fallen and the sun had come out. It was very cold, clear, and quiet, as the snow muffled sounds and few if any cars were out and about. Plows were finally starting to pass by and people were shoveling out their homes as I walked to work. It was school vacation and kids sledded and built snowmen. I was able to get to the mill on time and went to my regular assignment. As workers were able to get to work machines would turn on and cloth began to get made.

Shortly after I arrived, Tom Kenny came by and asked me if I could help out in a weaving room. They were short of workers and they needed me to help out. I was actually quite excited about the prospect.

I was handed over to the room supervisor who taught me on the spot how to be a bobbin boy or a battery hand. A bobbin girl, actually a woman in her late thirties or early forties, was the person I was filling in for and she was absent because she could not get to the mill due to the snowstorm.

On each loom on one side of the frame, over where the shuttle stopped after each run was made to get batted back again, was a metal cylinder called a battery. It was about eighteen to twenty-four inches in diameter and its purpose was to store bobbins filled with thread.

The battery held perhaps twenty or so bobbins, spring-loaded. When the bobbin in the shuttle was out of thread, a metal feeler would slide on the shiny bare wood rather than stay stationary if touching the thread. This would trigger an automatic insertion of a fresh bobbin. The expelling of the empty bobbin into a metal storage can below was an automatic action that took care of the spent bobbin.

The exchange of a new bobbin for an empty one was accomplished without missing a pick. The job of the battery hand was to push around a large wheeled bin of full bobbins and loom by loom, take a bobbin, unthread it a little, insert it with a brisk hand motion into the battery such that the spring-loaded mechanism held it in place, and take the thread and wrap it around a knob on one side of the cylinder-shaped battery. This last step was necessary in order for the thread to be free to unravel upon being inserted into the shuttle, and insured that when the shuttle flew back and forth the thread unraveled as it was supposed to.

Since the battery held twenty or more bobbins, the battery hand might be inserting quite a number of fresh bobbins for any given loom. The idea was to keep the battery well supplied so that the loom never stopped, at least not for lack of a full bobbin supply. The battery hand had to stay ahead of the weavers and would spend the whole day reaching deep into the bin if it was near empty or just off the brimming top if it was full.

It was mindless work that had to be done expeditiously.

So that was my job. Pick up a bobbin, thrust it into the spring hold, wrap the thread end around the center knob, and do it again and again. It was easy to do once shown, less easy to do fast, and a lot less easy to do after you'd been at it for a while. Soon the arms ache and the fingers get stiff. As the bin empties of bobbins one's back aches from repeatedly reaching three feet down, to fetch the last few bobbins. One does this for the whole shift and one aches all over.

I wondered if I'd even last out the shift. At about 11:00 a.m., after I had been a battery hand for four hours, the regular bobbin lady arrived covered with snow and smiling. The room was noisier now so she had to speak in a falsetto voice directly into my ear in order for me to understand her. "How did you like filling bobbins?" she asked. "Fine," I said. "I've been doing this for twenty years and I love it!" she exclaimed. "You don't have to think. I just lose myself in the rhythm of it and before I know it, it's time to go home." *So this is what being a textile worker is like,* I remember thinking to myself. Relieved, I wished her well as she took over.

I would not feel true relief until safely at home in a hot tub, later that afternoon. Maybe if I had worked as a battery hand every day I would have gotten used to it but while this job looked effortless it was backbreaking, at least for a neophyte, which I truly was.

19. My Last Work Shift.

My last work shift took place during spring vacation from college in 1954. I was to graduate from college in June and immediately commence service in the U.S. Navy as a commissioned naval officer. I was in the NROTC and military service was mandated in return for the naval training and partial scholarship afforded me by the navy along with a draft deferment for four years to complete college before service.

It was during this last workweek, or perhaps during Christmas vacation in 1953 when I also worked, that I observed a couple of the Boott Mills-designed corduroy-brushing machines sitting in the mill yard. They looked relatively new and yet there they were, sitting out in the mill yard in the rain, getting rusty.

I asked a supervisor about them and he told me they were to be picked up by the junk man. While I may not have had textile manufacturing, the Boott Mills, or the city of Lowell in my blood as much as my father did, seeing these relatively new machines being discarded brought on a sadness I still feel as I write this. George Breasth or his counterpart would soon be visiting the mill yard again, as I had seen him do in 1950, picking up cast-off machinery to be sold for its value as junk metal.

What was happening here? The mill was still packaging and selling corduroy under its own trademark but one more production step was moving to the southern mill because it could be accomplished more cheaply there than in Lowell Specifically, cutting and brushing were being done down there and the finished corduroy was being shipped to Lowell for dying, packaging, and sale. In my short and demarcated time at the Boott Mills, a school vacation week here, six weeks in the summer there, I had witnessed decreases in production, the closing of manufacturing floors, and the reduction of employees. The mill was becoming more ghost town than active plant right before my eyes.

In May 1954, the Boott Mills ceased production and it was liquidated a year later in 1955. My grandfather was eighty-eight in 1954 and he finally retired. He might have done this sooner (benefiting all?)

At this time my Uncle Frederick retired from active employment to transition into management consulting.

The Boott Mills plant and all its machinery was inventoried and sold. The new owners claimed that they were going to operate the mill, but everyone knew they wouldn't. In due course the machinery was sold to other plants or for scrap value. The new owners were mill liquidators, not operators and had a business record to prove it. The real estate was made available for lease. I recall that a laundry came in and some factory sales rooms. There may even have been an ice cream production company leasing space. This would take time. New England had empty textile mills along its rivers for most of the twentieth century. Cities like Lowell, Nashua, Manchester, Lawrence, Haverhill, Fall River, New Bedford, and many other smaller cities and towns had huge volumes of space, cheap, available, empty, and unwanted.

My father was hired by the new owners to be their representative for the same salary. He showed the space to prospective tenants, served as eyes and ears for the new owners and was available for consultation on operational issues having to do with the plant and equipment. He also knew Lowell and served as an informal and known interface between the new owners and the city and its officials. This arrangement bought him time. He was fifty-six years old. He said at the time that this job was not permanent. It was his for only as long as there was not a family member or close friend of the new owners who needed a job.

At that time my father had his second career crisis. (The first was an ongoing crisis in the relationship with his brother, which I will turn to later on.) With the mill sold, he had been able to "stop loss" with the caretaker job for the new owners, but was at pains to find something permanent.

He considered many things. Certainly he was interested in continuing in his industry if there were a suitable position and interest in a fifty-six-year-old executive. There wasn't any interest, which is not surprising given the demise of the textile industry in New England. He might have found employment had he been willing to relocate to the south, but my mother would never have left the city of Lowell, nor in fact would he. I believe relocation into a textile job was his first choice, but this was not to be. His passion for Lowell was stronger than his passion to remain in textiles by relocating to the south somewhere.

He also considered new careers. He had been active while

at Harvard College in the *Harvard Crimson*, the college daily, serving as business manager among other roles. Journalism on the business side with possibly a writing role was of interest and he mentioned journalism at this time, but I believe it remained a long shot without any activity or serious pursuit of a position that I know about.

However, this was not the case with the idea of becoming a lawyer. He actually corresponded with Suffolk University regarding entering law school. After his death I came across a file of this correspondence, which was amazing and very heartwarming to me. I had known of his night classes at the Lowell Textile School but he had never mentioned becoming a lawyer. In my own pursuit of a master's degree at night and on weekends, I felt I had been following in his footsteps.

His search for employment turned out well. He joined Samson Ocean Cordage Works as the purchasing agent. While not cotton textiles, making clothesline and other products was closely enough related. Samson was eventually bought-out by Enserch Corporation, the diversified energy company that had its headquarters in Texas. Samson Cordage followed the plastics craze and began producing polypropylene clotheslines as well as the cotton variety that we are all familiar with. However, Samson made much bigger, stronger rope and lines, including those used on merchant ships and smaller craft. In an especially noteworthy application they made a special line to attach to a spacecraft occupied by astronauts after it had parachuted into the Pacific Ocean. It had to be lifted from the water to the deck of an aircraft carrier by a helicopter. Enserch/Samson produced an ad using a picture of this space-related application of its product. Although Samson became Enserch, my father's employment continued until 1972, when he finally retired at age seventy-three.

The Samson office was located near South Station in Boston. My father continued his exercise routine, but did the walking in Boston instead of Lowell. Each day he would drive to the Lowell railroad depot, park in the yard, and take the train to North Station in Boston. Then he would walk from North Station to the Samson offices near South Station – about one mile. At day's end he would reverse his steps, walk the mile back to North Station, and take the train to Lowell.

PART 5: THE END OF THE MILL

20. OVERVIEW.

There are many learned studies of the demise of the New England textile industry. In the 1950s when I was in college, Seymour Harris, a distinguished Harvard economics professor, studied, wrote, and spoke about this industry and the causes and possible solutions for its problems. I took Harris' economics course and wrote a paper on the textile industry using my father as an informant. Readers seriously interested in this subject are of course better served by checking these academic and professional resources. (See Appendix for my father's treatment of the demise of the textile industry in Lowell.)

My interest, however, is two-fold. During my work in the mill, I witnessed the increasing effects of a dying business with each passing college term. The mill was shrinking. As I completed college, I went to work for a week or two at the mill here and there. During each stint at the mill, I noticed changes in production, for example, buying rather than producing grey goods. I noticed a shrinking production base as one room of looms after another was taken out of service, i.e., not heated, unoccupied, and destroyed. I wondered what management could do about this. Could management have been smarter? Management was my family. Did they make decisions that turned out badly? Did they not make decisions they could have made to prolong survival?

I remember reading a Harvard Business School type of study that said the best and the brightest people were drawn to certain industries, usually where new technology was most apparent and in use. The study correlated smarts with different industries and at the bottom were textiles. In other words, the textile industry could not attract the best and the brightest and/or the best and the brightest went elsewhere given a choice. Salaries also correlated and textile executives were paid substantially less than executives of other industries. Were my family members less than the best and the brightest and was I destined to be, or was I already, less than the best and the brightest? While my father never exerted any pressure on me to follow in his footsteps, at least in the 1940s and early '50s, it was still a choice. I used to think about this with great ambivalence. On the one hand, a dying industry was attractive seemingly only to those who had no other choices. On the other hand, a family business provided an opportunity for a clear shot to a top management position, a career choice if one enjoyed the fit and worked hard at it.

I stated above that I saw the mill going downhill unrelentingly. Yet I also saw the mill fight back and invest in itself. These decisions cost money and must have required substantial study and analysis before being approved and implemented. The three men involved were my father, my uncle, and my grandfather. My father used to talk about the greater efficiencies enjoyed by competing southern mills. I know that in the early years my grandfather made visits to southern mills. He was a director of the Merrimack Mills which had a mill in the south, but having a southern branch did not save the Merrimack Mills. In addition to paying lower wages and having no labor unions, the newer mills in the south were built on farmland where the production processes could be spread out and kept to just one floor or two. Furthermore, energy was cheaper. TVA rates were available to at least some of these mills. In addition, the mills would receive tax subsidies and abatements from the states where they were located. A recent PBS documentary on the textile industry noted that once the steam engine evolved enough to be used for generating electric power a textile mill could be located anywhere. It did not have to be located alongside rivers and streams that had drops over falls and rapids sufficient to create a "head" from which water power could cheaply produce power. Of course it made sense to build textile mills by fields where the cotton was grown when one could do so. Why would you ship cotton to Lowell, MA, when you could weave it a mile or so from where it was being harvested?

At the Boott Mills complex with nine mill buildings, each two to six stories tall, the production process started with railroad cars bringing raw cotton in at one end and then went up, then down, across bridges, around, back and down again into trucks picking up the finished product for delivery to customers. The ups and downs were by freight elevator and in some places ramps. The across was across passages built between mills at ground level and via bridges between the upper floors. The movement was largely by manpower. It took labor to take the work in progress (inventory) from one production step and move it to the start of the next production step. The warp threads and the bobbins had to meet in the weaving room for weaving. The finished cloth had to be taken to the bleachery and dye house and so on, all very inefficient by modern standards. It is no wonder these old mills stood vacant for so long. All this cheap space with high ceilings and huge floor-load capacity were in the final analysis increasingly less well suited for manufacturing. New industries were building new plants. Instead, I saw very small enterprises take clumps of space in the mills. Thus Lowell and similar textile communities languished for generations. Only in the last ten to twenty years have these old plants been converted into housing, offices, museums, restaurants on the river, etc. And there still is empty space available. The old mills serve these purposes well and I am sure communities are pleased to see an eyesore back on the tax rolls, but none of this provides jobs the way textile mills did. That kind of large economy/company town era is gone.

21. Plant Improvement and the Conveyor System.

In November 1949, in a statement to the directors, management reported "plant improvements which included three new water wheels and glass blocks in windows." In February 1949, management reported, "In 1948 it took steps towards a conveyor system for reducing the cost of departmental and interdepartmental handling of materials between processes. This has improved our internal transportation, eliminated some labor, reduced cost and speeded handling which reduces inventories. It is increasingly helpful and in time will help us even more" (Boott Records, Lowell Center for History, Box 37).

The Boott Mills started paying for the conveyor system in February, 1947. Although the Boott Mills was on strike from August 18, 1947 to April 16, 1948, it appears that the planning for the conveyor system continued unabated. Given the technical aspects of the conveyor system, I believe that my uncle Frederick must have played a major role in its planning and installation and that all three Flather managers and the board of directors signed off on the relatively sizeable investment required.

My father came back from a trip to the south having seen efficient one-story textile mills out in a former cotton field producing at half the cost of Lowell, MA. What to do? After World War II the Boott Mills invested in this large conveyor belt that snaked through virtually all nine mill locations and up and down all six floors. Large holes were cut in the floors so the conveyor belt could go from one floor to the next. The conveyor belt snaked its way from mill to mill at ground level and across the covered passageways higher up. A set schedule was maintained and at certain times in each shift, supplies, work in progress, partially manufactured goods, etc. would move faster, more easily, and more cheaply to the next location. In addition, at certain times during the day waste would be removed all according to the set schedule. The conveyor was huge and it was fully operational by 1950 when I started work.

The conveyor belt looked like a ski lift with a heavy-duty linked chain running fifteen feet or so off the floor on brackets from the ceiling from which different types of metal baskets or carrying rigs with hooks were attached, each type designed for the load it was transporting. The conveyor moved at a steady pace while still allowing loading and unloading as it went by. Was this kind of huge investment in infrastructure made in 1947-48 by a management that figured it would be around for a while? How do you explain this investment by a company that would soon be hemorrhaging money and totally out of business by 1954? Or if the future looked problematic was this huge investment seen as a way for the mill to better compete in the marketplace on a profitable basis by cutting labor costs? Clearly the conveyor belt was an example of modern technology being more cost effective than manual labor. When the conveyor belt became operational, laborers whose job it had been to push carts from one production process to the next were let go.

The full cycle of the conveyor belt took two and a half hours. This cycle included three floors in Building #1, three floors in Building #2, four floors in Building #3, five floors in Building #4, four floors in Building #5, five floors in Building #6, one floor in Building #7, one floor in Building #8, and three floors in Building #9.

The products moved included waste, cones, cans, roving, cloth, cans again, warp, boxes, filing, BL tow (towels), scrims, and laps.

Included in Appendix #4 is a photo of an industrial engineering guide for employees dated 5/23/51 which was produced as an aid to workers to schedule their conveyor assignments. The outer ring shows time elapsed up to twenty-two hours, the middle ring shows building and floor locations, and the inner ring shows products to be loaded on or off the conveyor system. A pin in the middle allowed the three rings to spin permitting one to calculate where the conveyor was at any given time and place. The guide was about one foot square in size, and the original which was in my possession was gifted to the National Historic Park Boott Mills Museum.

The conveyor system was 5,525 feet long and was powered by six drives. It became operational in 1949. After the mill closed out production in 1954, a complete machinery list was prepared by Werner Textile Consultants (Lowell Center for History, Boott Mills Papers, Box 51). This list inventoried every piece of equipment and machinery in the mill for use in disposal of this equipment, for use as designed (optimistic), or for use as junk value (realistic). The Lamson Conveyor System was valued at

$147,000, a tidy sum to spend in those days by a company facing severe competition with a strike underway and an uncertain future. Was this decision made by a management that did not innovate, did not seek to improve its competitiveness or build for the future? I think not. And furthermore this relatively large expenditure has been overlooked in all the textile books I have read about the Boott Mills. These books' authors were seemingly satisfied to describe management as "do nothing" while "seeking to improve." I hope to attract significant attention to the conveyor system because it was in fact the only practical option for the Boott Mills to turn a hundred-plus-year-old plant into the near physical equivalent of a modern one, a two-story southern mill.

I remember that there were difficult problems in the installation. One Sunday afternoon when I was fifteen or sixteen, I went to the mill with my father to check up on things. The conveyor chain had snapped during the past week and barely missed seriously injuring or even killing some workers. The stress on the chain was such that when broken, like the snap of a whip or the force of a broken anchor chain aboard ship, the force and speed of the flying ends of twenty or thirty feet of metal links could be lethal. Workers had to be able to move around the conveyor loading and unloading or just passing by without fear of being killed by flying chain. Also, the whole production process was now dependent on a smooth conveyor flow clearing supplies and products through the mill on a fixed schedule. Without the conveyor, the production process was shut down unless a manual labor fix could be put in place on the spot, a difficult thing to do with worker expectations, job descriptions, union rules, etc. By this time, the workers who used to wheel the bins of work in progress from one manufacturing step to another were mostly gone from the Boott Mills.

Thus, on this Sunday afternoon while the mill was closed and empty of people, a repaired conveyor belt was winding its way around the mill in a continuous loop. At various places a superstructure of wood packing crates had been assembled rising some ten or fifteen feet in the air off the floor which was reached by a set of stairs built for the purpose or by a ladder. On top were a couple of comfortable office swivel chairs in which sat mill maintenance and technical representative personnel and a factory representative from Lamson, the company that manufactured and installed the conveyor. They were looking through large TV magnifying glasses suspended from the ceiling on wires, inspecting each link in the conveyor chain for cracks or other signs of weakness. As it passed by, every link in the endless chain had to be inspected and reinspected. On Sunday the baskets were empty of product and the mill was empty of people. The next day, Monday, the mill would be full of workers and the baskets would be carrying regular loads adding to the stress on the linkages as designed. It had to work right. The anxiety level of everyone concerned was palpable. What had caused the break? Would there be a risk of future breaks? Were there other cracks in the chain links? Could further breaks be prevented? The stakes were high. My father was there on a Sunday to assure himself that all was going well so he could sleep that night, so that production schedules would be maintained, and so that the conveyor system would be operated with 100 percent safety for all workers.

22. THE END WAS AT HAND.

The Boott Mills managed to make a profit every year through 1952, but this positive record abruptly changed in 1953 when the entire textile industry went through a depression of sorts. The Boott Mills began to lose $50,000-$100,000 each month, and these losses continued into 1954 with no prospects for a change in the business outlook. By this time, as noted elsewhere, all production of cloth had ceased and finished cloth was being purchased from southern mills and packaged and sold as a Boott Mills product.

The directors did not wait long to express their pessimism for the future. They could invest their funds in any number of more profitable enterprises and pressure was placed on management to cut losses, end all production, sell out for the best price they could get, and pocket the proceeds. The mill ceased production in July, 1954, and was liquidated in 1955. The net worth at that time was around $1,250,000 meaning that the stockholders survived the closing with cash in hand. Stockholders received $130 for par value $100 stock. Frederick Ayer, F. Greg Bemis, and the combined Flather family interests each owned about 30 percent of the stock. The remaining 10 percent was publicly traded, but was never an active stock.

PART 6: FAMILY RETROSPECTIVES

23. Grandfather -- The Man on the Pedestal.

My grandfather, Frederick Arthur Flather, was born on March 21, 1867 in Nashua, New Hampshire, and lived to be one hundred years old. He worked until 1954, retiring at age eighty-eight when the Boott Mills ceased production. He was mechanically and technically inclined and owned and used a tool box in his earlier years. His father, Joseph, my great-grandfather, had migrated from Yorkshire, England where his family had been machinists. One can find the Flather name in telephone directories in England today. Grandfather was a member of several professional engineering associations and his work history was replete with evidence of technical expertise and interest. He started out as a blue-collar worker and rose to be a superintendent of works and finally a treasurer which was tantamount to being the chief executive officer.

Joseph, my great-grandfather, was born in 1837 and migrated first with his own father to the United States.

Landing in Baltimore in the 1850s, they moved around for a while, but finally came to Nashua, New Hampshire, where Joseph established the Flather Machine Shop. The remaining brothers and sisters followed in later years. As far as we can tell, all the Flathers in the United States today are related to this one family that came to Nashua one hundred and fifty or so years ago.

The machine shop made lathes among other things, and the logo of "F" followed by a diamond with "lathe" inside the diamond and an "R" at the other end spelling Flather always intrigued me. F-lathe-R. There are still Flather lathes around and my brother Newell owns one, as does my cousin Charlie.

Grandfather was twelve when the machine shop burned down and according to the family story he had to leave school and go to work. He told the story of receiving only an orange for Christmas. Later he worked for the Pettee Machine Works in Newton Upper Falls, MA, and built up quite a reputation as a machinist. At age twenty-two he was made superintendent at Pettee, although his father at the time thought it might have been better if it had waited two or three years.

Pettee was the first machine shop in the United States to recognize the merits of the English revolving flat card, to commence building it, and to distribute it to textile mills nationwide (*Boston Journal of Commerce*, Vol. 36, No. 16, January 24, 1891).

At that time, the industrial revolution had moved west and machinists were in high demand. Manufacturers like MacCormack Reaper and Deere Company would send recruiters east offering big dollars to engineers/machinists willing to relocate. My grandfather resisted these offers initially. He had a family, having married my grandmother in 1897. His first wife died of tuberculosis and he was thus widowed with one child, Drusilla. Finally in 1901 he succumbed to the MacCormack offerings and moved to Chicago to become superintendent of the works.

My father remembered going to the MacCormack estate on several occasions to attend birthday parties and play with the MacCormack children. Apparently my grandfather was high enough up in the MacCormack hierarchy to be invited to MacCormack parties and expected to attend, but he was low enough in the hierarchy to report to work on time the next day. Sometime in 1904 or 1905 he became ill and the decision was made to leave the employ of the MacCormack family and its presumed riches and to return to Massachusetts.

Before he did, however, he was on hand for the merger between the MacCormack and John Deering companies which became the International Harvester Company. Despite the positive aspects of the merger, there were contentious family issues as to shares of ownership and control such that grandfather was dispatched to supervise a security force guarding a lumber stockpile. There was an indication that the stockpile was the difference between control of the new company by one of the different families and it was important to make sure that the lumber pile remained undamaged. Accordingly, with his security force my grandfather stood on guard all night to make sure that the lumber stockpile survived until the next day when the final agreements of the merger were signed. According to the story, had the MacCormack lumber supply been torched, percentages of ownership and/or control would be changed definitively in disadvantage to the MacCormack interests. I suppose the MacCormack merger was not unlike many mergers today, with agreement at the top, but leaving hundreds or thousands below in the ranks to sort out or be sorted out over time.

At this time, Jacob Rogers, my grandmother's father, a

notable figure in Lowell having sat on the boards of eight of the textile mills in the city, wanted his daughter Alice, my grandmother, back home.

The Boott Mills had been closed since 1904. Jacob Rogers and a consortium of others had raised money to reopen the Boott Mills, and his son-in-law Frederick would be brought back from Chicago to run it. This happened in 1905. Frank Dunbar, Jacob Rogers' other son-in-law, handled all the legal aspects of the reopening of the Boott Mills.

My grandfather thus became treasurer of the Boott Mills. In the textile organization of the last century, the treasurer was the chief executive officer in charge of production, daily operations, and profit. The president of the company was the president of the board of directors. That position and ones like it at other companies were filled by the likes of Frederick Ayer and F. Greg Bemis, director of the Boott Mills.

Frederick Ayer was an industrialist and investor who gave the town of Ayer its name and also gave land for the army base at Fort Devens. F. Greg Bemis was responsible for importing huge quantities of jute from southeast Asia, notably Bangladesh (then part of Pakistan). We knew them as Bemis bags made out of burlap or jute in which potatoes or onions were often packaged.

24. The Sons, Roger and Frederick
-- Something Awful Happened.

My father, John Rogers Flather, was born on March 6, 1899. One year later to the day, on March 6, 1900, his brother, Frederick Flather, Jr., was born. The two boys, one year apart, were raised together and my grandfather often referred to them as "the boys" even when they were adults. My father attended Lowell High School and was sent off to Phillips Academy at Andover for his last two years. World War I was under way and he dropped out of Andover to join the National Guard. He served in the field artillery on the islands in Boston Harbor for less than a year and then was discharged in December, 1918. His brother Frederick also attended Andover and they graduated together. However, because of his military service, my father lacked credits to receive his high school diploma and attended summer school to make up for the lost school work. My father applied to MIT and was admitted and also to Harvard, but was not admitted initially. He and my grandfather went to Cambridge to meet with the Harvard administration. In due course with suitable explanations for military service commitments having precluded a high school diploma, and the make-up work of summer school, he was admitted to Harvard.

Brother Frederick, not serving in the military although he had applied, graduated in time for his high school diploma in 1919, and they both entered Harvard in September of 1919 and graduated in 1923.

That summer, as a graduation present I suspect, they traveled around the United States for several weeks playing every different golf course they could get to. Returning home, they began work at the Boott Mills in July of 1923. Father was 23; Frederick was 22.

Like I did years later, they worked in the mill proper in apprenticeship roles to learn the ropes and they received no salary for the first six months. My father took night courses at the Lowell Textile School, as did Frederick. I recall going with him to the Lowell Textile School years later on open-house days. This would have been in the 1930s and I would have been six or seven years old. What was distinctly memorable was a herd of sheep kept in a room indoors which were used to teach students how to shear wool. If there was a wool city it would have been Lawrence, but Lowell did have some wool production. Lowell was predominantly about cotton, though, and that is what my father studied. Lowell Textile School had to teach both cotton and wool production to its students to fully and adequately cover the field of textile manufacturing.

At some point, the brothers completed their apprenticeship and were elevated to management and moved to the front office. My grandfather remained treasurer as aforesaid. My father and Frederick were made assistant treasurer and assistant manager respectively in 1931. Frederick concentrated on technical and engineering questions and production. Father concentrated on marketing, sales, personnel administration, and labor relations.

Important decisions by their very nature had to be shared with the brothers presenting their ideas and recommendations to their father for a final determination. It is not clear whether the brothers were ever truly independent enough of their father to run the mill in Lowell on their own, and the fact that the brothers increasingly did not get along well only seemed to increase their dependency on their father.

My father and his brother Frederick lived at home until each was married. Father was married in 1928. While he and my mother were on their honeymoon in Europe, my grandfather and grandmother decorated the house next door to them. My grandfather lived at 68 Mansur Street and my home was next door at 52 Mansur Street. When Frederick married Edith Charles of New York City in 1927, my grandfather built a house for them up on the hill at 100 Belmont Avenue. All three houses still stand in good condition, and my home and my grandparents' home are in the Belvedere Hill Historical District in Lowell. I remember my cousins coming to early birthday parties. At one party they gave me a very nice sailboat for a gift. I can still see my cousin Charlie at the gate holding the boat. How old he was I don't know, perhaps five or six or seven. By 1937, the Fredericks, as we called them, had moved to Andover. They did not like living in Lowell and concluded that Andover's schools were superior to Lowell's. By all accounts they thrived in Andover. Uncle Frederick commuted by car each day, having lunch on many days with his mother at 68 Mansur Street.

My father had lunch downtown or walked home for lunch. His time to visit his mother and father was after work before dinner. I will forever hear my mother complaining that my father was going next door just when dinner was ready to be served and the children were hungry. It never changed. Thus the two men had their separate relationships with their parents.

At Christmastime, each family celebrated separately with the grandparents. My family was always with my maternal grandmother on Christmas Eve. We would return home to Lowell Christmas afternoon, at which point grandfather and grandmother would come over and we would celebrate Christmas around dinnertime. By then we were invariably Christmased out, but we were polite and coped and enjoyed seeing our grandparents as tired as we felt.

On Christmas day, the Frederick family celebrated Christmas with my grandfather and grandmother and my grandmother's sister, my aunt May Dunbar. Thus at Christmas, the two families were separated and never saw each other.

Both families came together at Thanksgiving. It was the only time we saw our cousins, once a year at my grandfather and grandmother's house. It was awkward. Seeing your first cousins once a year was not enough contact for a close relationship to develop.

The two men, sometime in the 1930s, had a serious falling out and thereafter they established increasingly separate ways of life. There was no personal contact between them beyond the minimum required by the once a year Thanksgiving dinner with the grandparents. A clear division between work, when they had to be together and non-work when they did not, was maintained rigidly throughout my childhood and teenage years. The antipathy between the two men continued throughout their lives and affected the nine children of the next generation, resulting in a guarded atmosphere between the two sets of cousins. The two families were clearly separated by distance and minimal contact, but most relevant, my father and his brother were unable to improve their relationship during their lifetimes, and the family situation was thus a stand-off until they died.

As we grew older, we began to run into our cousins socially. I was in the same class at Harvard as my cousins Charles and Frederick. My older sister Kitsey would run into her cousin Edith at parties. My sister Betsey and brother Newell would meet up with Drusilla. Then there were weddings and funerals when we saw our cousins. Meanwhile, my father preached good will to all people, what a strong family we came from, and other pieties. As we matured, observed, questioned, and drew our own conclusions, we took our parents' side instinctively which is what one would expect children to do. We did not have enough contact with our Frederick cousins to know what to think, and I believe they felt the same way about us. The two families were very polite to each other at Thanksgiving until everyone got home and asked what that was all about. The myths fell away over the years to painful realities. There were a lot of ghosts here.

Given the social estrangement, how did Rogers and Frederick work together at the Boott Mills for twenty or so years successfully? This was the background for my own work experience in the mill.

I actually got a whiff of it early on when I was perhaps ten years old. On a mill visit with my father, I was with him in his office for a short time one Saturday or Sunday afternoon. It was around 4:30 or 5:00 p.m. The mill was very quiet and no one was around except the usual after-hours watchmen, who turned on the lights in the office area after opening the gate across the road to let us in the mill yard. Father was there to do the usual one more thing. This was not a day to tour the plant. Grandfather's desk was in a separate office that by this time looked very unused. His schedule typically was to go to the mill briefly in the early morning and then take the 9:17 a.m. train to Boston. He would spend all day in the Boston office, returning to Lowell on a train that departed between 4:30 and 5:00 p.m. As treasurer, his operating responsibilities were to handle the company's cash, maintain bank relationships, and buy cotton, which he did from Boston for years. His Lowell office always seemed to look under-used. It was clean and neat that day. My grandfather also served on various boards of directors and would attend the directors meetings in Boston.

My father and Frederick shared an office next door that had two very large desks pushed together in the center of the room. The room was painted a pale green. With chairs on each side, they sat looking at each other face to face, perhaps mistrustingly, five days a week. This went on from some time in the mid 1930s to 1954. Twenty years give or take is a long time.

I recall that Uncle Frederick had a special telephone. It cried out to be picked up, examined, and experimented with. It was a regular telephone fitted with a large attachment that fit on the speaking end like a round ball perhaps six inches in diameter. The attachment had an opening to speak into so that when talking your mouth fit snugly into it, and all one could hear in the room would be muffled sounds. In other words, you could talk in privacy.

Of course I picked it up and wanted to try it out, and so my father nervously described how it worked. For me to hear the muffled sounds he had to do the talking. Then it was my turn to talk into it. I was intrigued, to say the least. I had never seen such a device and I haven't since. Then he told me to put it down as he glanced nervously at the door expecting Uncle Frederick to walk in at any moment and then there would be hell to pay. It seemed that my father took great pains to prevent any unnecessary altercations, and I suspect Frederick behaved in the same fashion. Mind you, it was late on a Saturday or Sunday afternoon and Frederick was probably safely occupied ten miles away at home in Andover. In any case my father was fearful of an altercation if Frederick witnessed him allowing his son to play around with his private phone. I came away with the feeling that Father gave Frederick a lot of space, yet they had to agree on almost everything operational at the mill. Disagreements or at least different points of view had to be discussed almost daily. Each of them therefore had to communicate effectively with the other on whatever subject was at hand.

It is hard for me to imagine how each man put up with this situation for so many years. Clearly their wives had to deal with the stress brought home and the children too were affected. Today, the nine grandchildren deal with it. It was not our fault, but we had to deal with it. While I did side with my father as children always do at least for a while, I did not like the pain. I did not like carrying this heavy family trip around like a brick. I felt early on that Rogers was more right and Frederick was more wrong, but that conclusion increasingly failed to work for me. What good did it do if each set of cousins remained on opposite sides? A more realistic conclusion is that both brothers were at fault and both were responsible for rupturing a normal fraternal relationship. My feeling today is that we all have our own lives to lead and it is better to improve communication and relationships and to shed these family ghosts if we can.

To our collective credit as cousins, everyone has tried to reach across the divide. We can look forward to the rest of our lives, we can enjoy each other's company, and we can seek the others out at weddings, funerals, reunions, trips, and parties. We can enjoy talking about our family's heritage. Cousins are flesh and blood. Cousins matter. We are one family!

My cousins and siblings are as much at a loss as I am. Today we treasure indications that at some basic level the brothers, despite their animosity, felt some feeling of friendship, respect, and love for each other at least near the end. When I had lunch some years ago with my cousin Frederick III, Uncle Frederick's oldest son, he took me to the office in Andover he shared with his father until his father died. Frederick III showed me his father's checkbook and written on the stub page for Sunday, October 28, 1979, was "Rogers died today." That simple statement reassured each of us that some caring for the other existed between them, and we hugged each other warmly on departure.

My parents also professed to be at a loss as to the cause of the break in relations. They told me that Uncle Frederick and Aunt Edith did not wish to live in Lowell and seemed much happier after the move to Andover. Clearly something happened. Perhaps my father did or said something or my mother did or said something that so angered Uncle Frederick and Aunt Edith that they pulled down the curtain on any kind of close relationship. I will never know, nor will my siblings and my first cousins.

Then again, the growing animosity and lack of trust between the brothers may have accumulated incrementally over time, building on disagreements, misunderstandings, perhaps even competition at the mill for their father's approval. The poor relationship between the brothers put tremendous stress on both of them. Every decision and every meeting had to be carried out with the ghost of a sour personal relationship hovering over them.

Where were my grandfather and grandmother in this? In denial above the fray it appears. Perhaps such detachment in family relationships went with the times.

My grandfather was self-made. He did not attend college and did not even graduate from high school. He did attend night school in drafting and accounting at Bryant and Stratton and business school in Boston. He was a workaholic, going to work every day until he was eighty-eight. If the mill hadn't closed in 1954 he might have continued to work longer. Where was he? Did he try to mediate? It appears not. It appears that he never sat down to talk about the relationship between the three of them. My father never mentioned his own father in any discussions about his problems with his brother. My father revered his father, as I believe Uncle Frederick did. They seem to have treated their father like a hero and placed him on a hero's pedestal. If my father ever thought ill of his father, he never said anything. It's as if he had purged himself of any negative thoughts or concerns. There was a blind loyalty there. In 1970, when my grandmother died and the house at 68 Mansur Street was being closed out and sold, the family had meetings around the disposal of the furniture. However, once my grandmother was gone and all assets disposed of, the two brothers were finally free of each other. There were virtually no ties left. The Thanksgiving holiday dinners ended as my grandparents aged and were not resumed after their deaths. No family gatherings or meetings were desired or scheduled thereafter. The only contact between the brothers involved occasional joint meetings of a family trust for which each was a trustee along with a bank. For many years, the only contact between the two sets of parents and grandchildren was at weddings, funerals, and accidental meetings such as I would have with my two cousins at Harvard.

Thank heavens it is different now that the children are in their sixties and seventies. We have reached out, enjoyed being together, enjoyed talking about our heritage, and yes, enjoyed patching up the fissures.

The two brothers also had different priorities regarding the role of a possible fourth generation at the mill and regarding the city of Lowell generally. As noted earlier, my father was jubilant about my working at the mill as an apprentice whether or not I wanted to make my work relationship there permanent. The mere fact that I started work in 1950 at age seventeen made him a very proud and happy man.

As it turned out, I was the only member of the fourth generation to work at the mill. My two cousins, Frederick III and Charles, never worked at the mill and never visited their father's office or toured the production areas as I had done so many times. As each of my male cousins told me, "Father did not want us in the mill." The fact that Frederick moved to Andover and commuted each day to Lowell for work pretty much precluded any easy or convenient mill visitation plan for his sons.

It follows that my father and mother had a much stronger and understandable stake in the city of Lowell and its affairs than Uncle Frederick and Aunt Edith did. Once they moved to Andover, they were engaged in local activities there and Lowell was relegated to just a place where Frederick commuted to each day for work.

In sum, Lowell was a passion for my parents, while for my aunt and uncle it was a place they had chosen to leave behind other than during work hours for my uncle. The two men had chosen their separate ways, as had their spouses, and nothing in the management of the Boott Mills was going to change that. They coped somehow or other.

I have concluded that circumstances at the Boott Mills and the personal attributes of my father and uncle were such that my father likely enjoyed the better fit with the mill. My father always wanted to be a businessman and always wanted to work in manufacturing. Working in Lowell, a big part of his passion in life, and being part of a family business were added pluses. His responsibilities for marketing, sales, personnel administration, and labor relations were well within his interests and capabilities. He was called upon daily to perform functions and make decisions regarding one or more of these areas. His skills and interests were fully utilized.

My uncle Frederick, on the other hand, had strong interests and skills in engineering and technology which in cotton textile manufacturing were only intermittently used. To be fair, he was fully motivated and occupied when the Boott Mills purchased new state-of-the-art machinery such as long-spinning, high-speed looms. He was also called upon when the production process was vertically integrated by installing a bleachery and entering the finishing of corduroy, both requiring new machinery and plant layout. In addition, he must have had a major role in the planning and installation of the new conveyor system which sought to modernize an old plant. However, once these major improvements and innovations were completed, his daily routine was oversight of the production power which in cotton textile manufacturing is pretty straightforward. The Boott Mills departmental supervisors were highly skilled and experienced in their specialties and served in these positions for many years. There was little if any turnover.

Engineering job offers came to the Boott Mills for the services of my uncle, but he was never informed and only learned of them later when it was too late to act upon them. My grandfather seems to have been involved somehow according to some business protocol and stepped in to deny his second son the opportunity of at least considering one or more challenging positions. This is not to say that my uncle Frederick would have left the family business, but in employment terms, having a choice is key even when the decision as often as not may be to reselect the present job. Either way, my uncle Frederick, I believe, would have been a happier man had he been given the opportunity to consider engineering positions outside the Boott Mills. One could conclude that there was a controlling side of my grandfather that I never saw as a grandchild and never heard discussed at home, ever. We kids seem to have placed my grandfather on the same high pedestal that his two sons did, and why not? That's what we were told to do.

25. St. Joseph's Hospital School of Nursing - My Mother's Place in Lowell, Massachusetts.

My mother's role as wife of a mill manager living in Lowell involved her substantially in the life of the city. She enjoyed this role, was well prepared for it, and was oriented towards maximum involvement. Her focus was the well-being of women, girls, and children. Although she would never have used the term herself, she was in fact an early feminist and was in touch with the values and objectives of the women's liberation movement which started in the 1950s.

Sometime during the 1950s she was asked to serve on the board of directors of St. Joseph's Hospital School of Nursing, an appointment she readily accepted. My father was then serving as a trustee at the Lowell General Hospital and their efforts in the health care field complimented each other. They were able to provide each other with mutual support and they enjoyed working on health projects in Lowell. My mother often talked about the strong affinity she felt with the nuns who ran the school of nursing. She enjoyed being with them and felt she had a strong rapport with them.

However, my mother always wondered why she was asked

to serve in this capacity when there were, as she said, "many qualified and prominent French Canadian and/or Catholic women in Lowell whom you'd expect would have been chosen for a Catholic hospital run by French Canadian nuns." The only explanation she could ever come up with was that her appointment may have been connected somehow or other with a decision made by my grandfather in 1930 to keep the hospital in existence.

On November 1, 1839, ten textile corporations under the umbrella of the Properties of the Locks and Canals on Merrimack River entered into an article of agreement (see Appendix 2) to establish the Lowell Hospital Association. The agreement outlined the establishment and maintenance of a hospital in Lowell, "for the convenience and comfort of persons employed by the ten mills, when sick or needing medical or surgical treatment." The treasurers of the ten corporations created a board of trustees to oversee the association, which in turn appointed a board of trustees to oversee the affairs of the hospital, hire staff, manage accounts, and make timely reports of effectiveness.

While any given textile mill could opt out at any time provided its payments were current, it would do so by waiving its share of any ultimate distribution of assets should the hospital cease to exist.

On the other hand, the dissolving of the association required the unanimous vote of all member corporation treasurers (see Article 15, Appendix 2).

Thus, the textile mills met the health care needs of workers by operating and paying for their own hospital. This situation continued until 1930 when the mills concluded that sufficient health care, including hospitals, had been created in Lowell by the private sector, so that it was no longer necessary for them to pay for a corporation hospital.

The mill treasurers met in 1930 with the objective of closing the hospital and selling off all assets. The Pawtucket Street location was especially attractive to real estate interests and the mill treasurers saw a tidy profit coming from the sale of this property. One of the interested parties, according to my father, was a gas station.

Although my grandfather agreed that the mills should no longer operate their own hospital, he did not agree that the hospital should cease to exist. He felt that the hospital was a community asset that effectively served a large population and that the mills should find someone else to own and run it.

Article 15 of the agreement required a unanimous vote to dissolve the hospital association and close the hospital. My grandfather's dissenting vote was the only one among the group. The treasurers then decided to give the association trustees a year to find another group to run the hospital.

It appears from the record that the mill leadership initially tried to sell the hospital to the Catholic Church for $70,000, but there was no agreement for paying for a community asset that the community felt should be theirs for free.

In due course, the hospital was sold for one dollar to the Oblate Fathers who in turn brought in the Grey Nuns (Soeurs Grise de laCroix) from Ottawa, Canada. According to my family's recollections, the nuns had a year to prove themselves worthy of running the hospital, but there was never any question of their dedication and capabilities. The renamed St. Joseph's Hospital was a success from the outset and continued to serve Lowell for many years. Health care is still administered from the Pawtucket Street location, although this hospital has been part of the health care reorganization that has occurred nationwide. Today it is part of the multi-site complex known as Saints Memorial Medical Center.

I believe my mother served on the board of directors of the nursing school until 1969 when it decided to close. This decision was made in response to changing health care requirements taking place in the region. Hospital-based three-year schools of nursing were being replaced by four-year colleges granting nursing degrees.

The single opposing vote of my grandfather to retain the mill association hospital was a matter about which he was most proud. This story was often told in the family. Whether or not there was any true connection between his vote to save the hospital and my mother's serving on the board, it is safe to say that she felt a true dedication to St. Joseph's Hospital School of Nursing and the group of nuns who ran this school so well for so many years. She often said, "Maybe St. Joseph's Hospital was trying to thank the family (i.e., Grandfather) for his dissenting vote and the effort that followed to find the Canadian nuns to run the hospital for the foreseeable future so successfully." On the other hand, perhaps there was no discernible connection to my grandfather's vote and she was chosen to be a board member of the school of nursing on her own merits. My father tended to support this latter view believing that her many community activities qualified her for any number of service organization boards, especially those concerned with the well-being of women and children.

26. THE BOSS'S SON -- SETTING THE RECORD STRAIGHT.

Up to this point in this memoir the reader could conclude that my father and I were close as father and son, especially in the context of the Boott Mills. That is true. We enjoyed our shared experiences at the mill and discussed them together.

However, the Boott Mills experience was only a part of the totality of a father-son relationship, and in other areas I was often at odds with my father.

Our best communication and most satisfying moments together involved those times when we mutually enjoyed discussions, such as about my service in the U.S. Navy as a career pilot. My father was proud of his military service, short as it was. My mother strongly opposed my flying and my father preferred to take the train whenever possible and probably took less than five commercial flights in his life. However, he always wanted to talk with me about my own flying experiences whenever he could. We climbed a number of mountains together while on vacation in New Hampshire and those were memorable experiences too.

The Peace Corps was even more germane to a close relationship. At one time, my father had two sons in the Peace Corps. My brother Newell was a member of Ghana #1, the first group of volunteers to go overseas, and I was on the staff in the Philippines, and later Malaysia and Micronesia. My sister Betsey was on the selection staff of the Vista Program in Washington, D.C. Sargent Shriver, first director of the Peace Corps and later director of the Office of Economic Opportunities Program, selected my father as a "domestic volunteer" to head up all speaker bureau activities in Eastern Massachusetts for the Peace Corps. He and my mother spoke perhaps once a week on average for more than five years. I have wonderful memories of my family's efforts to collect and send books to Ghana for my brother's school library. I also have good memories of the discussions we had about the Peace Corps during my consultation trips to Washington, D.C. and during brief vacations when transferring to new country assignments.

These were pluses in a relationship that otherwise was often characterized by tension brought on by his seemingly excessive preoccupation with family appearances, sometimes to the detriment of the feelings of the individual family member involved. He and my mother seemed more interested in parading the five of us around like puppets rather than just having us along as a family group.

My father grew up in a Victorian household that placed much emphasis on the importance of outward appearances in behavior. His constant preaching about conservative behavior and his caution, even fearfulness, filled the spaces between our occasional discussions about the Boott Mills, the navy, and the Peace Corps. Over a number of years I dealt with this tension by separating myself as much as possible without ever explaining why. I achieved for myself a certain private space where I could lead a life opposite to Victorian values. My rebellion lasted longer than a normal adolescent's rebellion. In the process, I lived very much apart from my parents. This also included living apart from my siblings, through no fault of their own.

In time, I came to the realization that this attitude was not very helpful to me because my anger often clouded what should have been mature judgment. I began to make a transition back to the family and went to each of my siblings to explain how I felt and apologize. My behavior over the years had nothing to do with them. I am grateful to them for accepting me back. It remained for me to approach my father and tell him how I had felt for many years and to apologize to him, too. I wanted to build a happier and more compatible father-son relationship. By the time I was ready to talk with him it was too late. He had become a dying man with Alzheimer's disease. After he died I talked with my mother who told me that my father was always very proud of me and loved me very much. Today, I am a proud son and love my father's memory.

27. Becky - Fifty-five Years Together and Counting.

Becky and I met at her sophomore prom on May 15, 1949. We were both fifteen years old. I never dated another girl.

We were married on June 25, 1954, right at the time that the Boott Mills was closing for good, and immediately thereafter I began military service with the U.S. Navy. I would not enter the Boott Mills again until it had become the central piece of the Lowell National Historical Park many years later, and the home of the Boott Mills Cotton Textile Museum.

Our four children were born between 1955 and 1964 and their lives thus came after the period of 1937-1954 covered by this book. However, they had significant input into this book, especially the family retrospective chapters. Their memories, experiences, and perspectives regarding their grandparents were very helpful to me.

Becky was on hand when I began working at the Boott Mills in 1950, and her insights permeate this book.

There have been two important advantages of my getting cancer. The first is that cancer gave me more time, motivation, and determination to do some writing. This book has become my cancer-fighting morale booster.

The second advantage of cancer concerns my relationship

with my immediate family. These relationships have deepened and become more intimate and have been vital to my meeting the battle of cancer head on. Today I am a truly loved man.

28. Interview with Retired Workers - Miss Gilman Revisited.

In 1974, while working at the Educational Development Center in Cambridge, Massachusetts, I had the opportunity to participate in interviewing several textile workers in Lowell, Massachusetts, as part of a curriculum development project. I asked my father to arrange a tour of the locks and canals of Lowell for the working party and also a meeting with former textile workers for a discussion of their work in the mills and life afterward. EDC had a people and technology course under development. It contained a whaling unit, an African unit, and several other units under discussion. Additional units were planned, possibly including among other things the New England textile industry.

My supervisor and several others toured the locks and canals in Lowell in a downpour. We went to the Francis Gate and we also went down some steep steps in a dam at the falls at the Pawtucket Gate, where I had never been before. After this most interesting tour we met at my parents' home with three textile workers, the famous Miss Jennie Gilman, Miss Sadie Swett, and Mr. Joe Higgenbottom. All were quite elderly at this point, in their 80s, and very sharp. Joe Higgenbottom had the most to say. He talked happily and comfortably about his career at the Boott Mills. He had been a supervisor. Most interesting, he talked about wanting to become a doctor and interviewing at Boston University to determine how many pre-med courses he had to take in order to attend medical school. He had saved up enough money to afford one year of school but not two, as the university required, so he gave up on his doctor ambitions. He was not angry, disappointed, or bitter. That was just the way things were then. He remained in his textile career at the Boott Mills. He also talked about the many theater performances he gave, having a lifetime interest in the theater, and he remarked about how dramatic the change was when electricity replaced gas lamps in his home in Lowell. It was a very upbeat interview.

Miss Swett, the oldest, said little beyond positive statements of support for the Flather family and her employment for so many years at the Boott Mills.

Miss Gilman, ever true, brooked no negativity or criticism of the Boott Mills or the Flather family. She was asked to tell us about her memories which she did happily including her worst as well as her best recollections. She answered the question about her bad memories by saying that there were no bad memories; everything was good. She used the word "loyal" happily when referring to her style, her time at the Boott Mills, and her feelings about working with the Flather family. True to her life cause, Miss Gilman must have gone to her grave without ever deviating from being the steady, steely, efficient, accomplished, confident employee who had charge of the payroll, the personnel functions of the company, and the private records. She said she worked for the Flather family and the Boott Mills happily, loyally, agreeably and supportively. There was no other side. This certainly agreed with my recollections of her when I worked in the mill. I never heard my father say anything other than these things about her, and there would be no break in the recollection on this day in 1974. Miss Gilman was always pro-management.

She had great respect for my father. He had great respect for her. My father could not get along with his own brother, but he got along famously with Miss Gilman.

I thought back to my time at the mill and I remembered how she had tormented me and tried to shape me into her own image. I remember the humiliation I felt and I remember the bad press she uniformly received from just about all the employees in the mill. She had power over all the workers, and especially the supervisory staff, and she had power in special ways over my family. And on those fateful days back in 1950, she was making sure her power would extend to the next generation of Flathers should that include me.

Yet her role was vital and her performance crucial to the success of my family's management and operation of the mill.

I could now see both sides of Miss Gilman, my family's side and the workers' side. Miss Gilman had just one role to play and she played it successfully throughout her career. There could be no other way. She had no other choice. You have to respect her for the dedication, loyalty, and perfection she brought to the task, knowing all the while I'm sure that some people disliked her and resented her power. It is proper and fair for her to have the last word. In retrospect, I admire and respect Miss Gilman deeply and understand fully what her job description was and how vital it was to the Boott Mills and the Flather family for her to be, well, "Miss Gilman." She deserves the last word.

APPENDICES

Appendix I – Spindle City

THE ORIGIN OF THE CITY OF SPINDLES

Mr. Nathan Appleton of Boston, in a recent letter, gives the following account of the first undertaking at Lowell.

As connected with this fact, and as constituting the germ of the present city of Lowell, the following circumstances may be thought interesting. Mr. Patrick T. Jackson and myself had been amongst the original associates who established the Boston Manufacturing Company of Waltham, in which the power loom was first brought into successful operation on this side of the Atlantic. The success of that establishment had satisfied us that the time had arrived for undertaking the manufacture and printing of calicoes, and the summer of 1821 we made an excursion into New Hampshire in search of a suitable water power.

Soon after our return, the idea was suggested to Mr. Jackson of purchasing the stock of the Pawtucket Canal on the Merrimack River, together with such lands as might be necessary for using the great water power which might be created by its enlargement. He communicated the same to me. After ascertaining that Mr. Kirk Boott was willing to join us in the enterprise, and become the agent or manager to carry it into effect, we proceeded through trusty agents to purchase the canal and the most important adjoining lands. It was not until these had been secured, that we thought it proper to visit the scene. I well recollect the visit. It was in the month of November, 1821, and a slight snow covered the ground. The party consisted of Mr. P. T. Jackson, Kirk Boott, Warren Dutton, Paul Moody, John W. Boott and myself. We perambulated the grounds and scanned the capabilities, and it may be worth recording that so sensible were we of its future importance, that I distinctly recollect the remark made by one of the party, that some of us might live to see the place contain 20,000 inhabitants. We proceeded with new associates to organize the Merrimack Manufacturing Company, with a capital of $600,000, to which corporation the whole property was conveyed. The enlargement of the canal was finished during the two following summers, and on or about the 1st day of September, 1823, the first water-wheel performed its revolutions. The city now contains, I am told, upwards of thirty thousand inhabitants.

I certainly look back with pleasure and satisfaction upon the part which I have had in leading to this result. I do not say this with any reference to pecuniary interest. I could not say it, did I not conscientiously believe that the introduction of the cotton manufacture has added greatly to the mass of human happiness in those immediately concerned in it, as well as to the aggregate wealth and prosperity of the whole country. I could not say it, did I perceive in the system any tendency toward a relaxation of the moral purity which has ever been a characteristic of our beloved New England. My mind was early turned to a consideration of this question. I could never perceive any just ground for the opinion which formerly prevailed extensively, that occupation in manufactories was less favorable to morals than other manual labor. This opinion has, I believe, universally given way before the light of experience. It is the elevation of labor above the right of a mere subsistence, which gives it character and standing in society, and constitutes the elementary difference between American and European labor. That this elevated position may be strengthened and perpetuated by our institutions is my ardent wish.

Source

Daily Herald

Vol. XV, Newburyport, Wednesday Morning January 27, 1847. No. 179 (author's files)

APPENDIX II – ARTICLES OF AGREEMENT OF THE LOWELL HOSPITAL ASSOCIATION

ARTICLES OF AGREEMENT

OF THE

LOWELL HOSPITAL ASSOCIATION

NOVEMBER, 1839

BOSTON: - CASSADY AND MARCH,

No. 8 Wilson's Lane......Up Stairs

1839.

Articles of Agreement, made and executed this first day of November, in the year of our Lord eighteen hundred and thirty-nine, by and between the Proprietors of the Locks and Canals on Merrimack River, - the Merrimack Manufacturing Company, the Hamilton Manufacturing Company, the Appleton Company, the Lowell Manufacturing Company, the Middlesex Company, the Suffolk Manufacturing Company, the Proprietors of the Tremont Mills, the Lawrence Manufacturing Company, the Boott Cotton Mills, and the Massachusetts Cotton Mills, - Corporations duly established by the Legislature of the Commonwealth of Massachusetts:

WHEREAS, the said Corporations have agreed to establish and maintain a Hospital, in the city of Lowell, in said Commonwealth, for the convenience and comfort of the persons, employed by them respectively, when sick or needing medical or surgical treatment; and have agreed to contribute the funds necessary for that purpose, as hereinafter set forth:

Now, the said Corporations do hereby declare, -- and each of them for itself, and not the one for the other or others of them, do hereby covenant and agree to and with each and every other party hereto, in manner and form as is hereinafter set forth, and that each of them will be subject to, and will observe and perform the several stipulations, terms, and conditions, contained in the following Articles, that is to say:

First. The Several Corporations, parties hereto, and such others as may hereinafter become their associates, shall be and continue an association, under the name of the *Lowell Hospital Association*, from the day of the date hereof until the same shall be dissolved in the manner hereinafter provided, -- but reserving to each of them the right to withdraw from the same, on the terms hereinafter expressed.

Second. The funds, necessary for the purchase of real estate, a hospital, and other suitable buildings, fixtures, furniture, and property, for said Association, shall be contributed, and paid to the Treasurer thereof by the respective parties hereto, and their associates, in proportion to their several capital stocks paid in: and the Treasurer of said Association shall deliver suitable receipts for all moneys so contributed and paid.

Third. The Treasurers, for the time being, of the several corporations, parties hereto, and of such other corporations as may hereinafter become their associates, shall be, ex officio, the representatives of them, respectively, in all things concerning the property and concerns of said Association, and the management thereof, with full power and authority, irrevocable, to do and cause to be done all things which they may deem needful or proper to effect the objects of the parties, and not repugnant to the terms or provisions of this instrument.

Fourth. The said Treasurers shall hold a meeting for the purpose of organizing their Board, within sixty days from the date of this instrument; and shall hold a meeting on the first Wednesday in June, in every year afterwards, at such time and place as a majority of them shall designate.

Fifth. The said Board of Treasurers shall elect a chairman to preside at its meetings; and, in his absence, a chairman pro tempore; also a clerk; -- and shall make such rules (not inconsistent with these articles) as it may deem proper for the regulation of its own proceedings. A majority of the Board shall constitute a quorum for the transaction of business; and all lawful acts may be done or authorized by a vote of a majority of the Board present at its meeting, provided a quorum be present. Whenever a quorum shall not be present, a majority of those present may adjourn the meeting to such time and place as they may determine. In case of any vacancy in the Board, all the powers and authority, conferred on the whole Board, shall be held and enjoyed by the remaining members thereof, or by a majority of them, until such vacancy shall be filled.

Sixth. The said Board of Treasurers shall elect, by ballot, twelve Trustees, and a Treasurer of said Association, who shall, ex officio, be a Trustee; each of whom shall hold his office during the pleasure of said Board. The said Board shall appoint, annually, or oftener, one or more physicians and surgeons, who shall have the direction of their respective departments subject to the orders of the Board of Trustees, and shall hold their offices, respectively, during the pleasure of that Board. The Board of Treasurers shall also appoint such consulting physicians and surgeons as may be needed in cases of difficulty or danger.

Seventh. The said Board of Treasurers shall purchase all such real estate as it may deem necessary for the purposes of said Association, and for such prices and on such terms as it may deem reasonable.

Eighth. All real estate, which may be acquired for said Association by purchase, or otherwise, shall be conveyed to the said "Proprietors of the Locks and Canals on Merrimack River," -- to be held by that corporation in trust, and for the objects, intents, and purposes herein expressed and contained, -- and subject to the direction and disposition of a majority of the Treasurers of the parties to this instrument as the same may be declared in writing. The orders, in writing, of a majority of said Treasurers, for the time being, concerning such real estate, or the sale, conveyance, or other disposition thereof, shall be sufficient authority for any and all acts which the said Proprietors may do, or cause to be done in pursuance thereof. And the said Proprietors shall not be held or required to cause any insurance or repairs to be made on any real estate or property of said Association, nor to pay any taxes thereon, nor to do any act whatever concerning the same excepting to hold the title thereto in trust as aforesaid, -- to convey the same by deed or deeds of release and quitclaim pursuant to said orders in writing,-and to make, execute, and deliver such declarations of trust, deeds, and other instruments relating to the real estate which said corporation may hold as aforesaid, as shall, from time to time, be requisite for the safety and management thereof, and the accomplishment of the objects of the Association, or for its final dissolution. And upon every conveyance of real estate to said corporation, to be held by it in trust for said Association, the said corporation shall endorse and execute upon the deed of conveyance, or otherwise make and execute, a sufficient declaration that such real estate is held by it upon the trusts herein expressed and contained. In all other respects, the said Proprietors shall be subject to the agreements, terms, and provisions contained in this instrument in the same manner as each of the other corporations parties hereto.

Ninth. The Trustees, elected as aforesaid, shall hold a meeting, without unnecessary delay after their election, for the purpose of organizing their Board;-shall elect a chairman to preside at its meetings--and in his absence, a chairman pro tempore,-also a clerk,--and shall make such rules, not inconsistent with these articles, as it may deem proper for the regulation of its own proceedings. The Trustees shall have the general superintendence, care, and management of the property and concerns of the association;-shall cause all needful repairs to be made in and about its buildings and real estate; and shall purchase all such furniture and other articles as they may deem necessary for the purposes of the Association, for such prices as they may deem reasonable.

The Board of Trustees shall meet at least as often as once in every month, at such time and place as they shall by vote designate: They shall appoint annually, or oftener, a superintendent of the Hospital, and such assistants and servants as they may deem necessary, and define their duties and fix their compensation: They shall make such rules and regulations for the government of the physicians, surgeons, superintendent, assistants, and servants, and concerning the admission of patients, and the management of the respective departments of the Institution, as they may deem needful and proper;-provided that such rules and regulations shall not be repugnant to these articles, and shall be subject to be altered, amended, or annulled by the Board of Treasurers, at their annual meeting, or at any meeting specially called for the purpose.

The Trustees shall exhibit to the Board of Treasurers, at every annual meeting thereof, a written report on the accounts of the Treasurer of the Association, and on the state of the Hospital, with a statement of the number of patients admitted and discharged during the year in each department, and statements of the receipts and expenditures in each department;-all which statements and reports shall be prepared under the direction of committee of the Trustees especially appointed for the purpose by their Board, which committee shall subscribe the same.

Tenth. The board of Trustees shall establish from year to year, an equitable rate of board to be paid by all patients who may be received into the Hospital; and every such patient shall pay his or her board accordingly, together with all expenses that may be incurred on his or her account;--excepting cases in which it may be otherwise specially agreed. And the corporation, in whose service the patient may be at the time of his or admission, or by request of whose agent he or she may be admitted, shall pay such board and expenses to the Treasurer of the Association whenever the patient shall fail to pay the same.

Eleventh. Whenever, at the end of any year, the expenses of the Institution shall be ascertained to have exceeded its receipts, such excess shall be paid on demand to the Treasurer of Association by the parties hereto and their associates, in proportion to their respective capital stocks paid in at that time.

Twelfth. The clerks, who may be chosen by the said Boards of Treasurers and Trustees respectively, shall notify and attend all meetings of their respective Boards, and keep full and true records of their doings in suitable books, which shall be the joint property of the corporations interested in the concern; shall be accessible to each of them, and their respective officers and agents at all times,--and shall be admissible evidence of all facts contained therein. In the absence of the clerk of either of the said Boards, his duties shall be performed by a clerk to be chosen pro tempore.

Thirteenth. The Treasurer of said Association shall keep, and dispose of, all its moneys, bonds, notes, and other valuable papers, pursuant to the directions of the Board of Trustees. He shall collect all moneys that may become due, and give suitable acquittances therefor. He shall pay no money except in pursuance of the order of the Board of Trustees, or its committees duly authorized by it to draw therefor, or in payment of the fixed salaries of the superintendent and others in the employment of the Institution. He shall keep a regular set of books, containing the accounts of the Association, and of all its funds that may pass through his hands. He shall make to the Boards of Treasurers and Trustees, respectively, such statements concerning the financial affairs of the Association, as either of them shall, from time to time, require; and shall make a complete settlement of the accounts and books to the last day of April, annually, and exhibit the same to the Board of Treasurers at its annual meeting; and he shall attend faithfully to all other duties, which the Boards of Treasurers and Trustees, respectively, may require him to perform.

Fourteenth. Either of the parties hereto, or of their associates, by its Treasurer acting in its behalf, may, at any time, withdraw from said Association, by giving to the Treasurer thereof written notice of an intention to do so: but in every such case, the corporation, so withdrawing, shall pay its proportion of all charges and expenses to the time of such withdrawal, and shall forfeit and release to the remaining and continuing members of the Association all its right, title, and interest in and to the Hospital and the real estate and property of the Association, and all benefit and advantage to be derived therefrom.

Fifteenth. The said Association may be dissolved whenever the Board of Treasurers of the respective corporations, members thereof, shall unanimously vote the same to be expedient: In which case all its real estate, personal property, and effects, shall be sold and disposed of at public auction, or private sale, at such times, in such manner, for such price or consideration, and on such terms and conditions, as a majority of the said Board shall direct: And the net proceeds of such sale or sales shall be divided and distributed between the corporations, then members of said Association, in the same proportions in which they shall have contributed to its funds and capital stock.

Sixteenth. Any other corporation or corporations may become members of said Association, and participate in the advantages thereof, on such terms and conditions as the Board of Treasurers may prescribe.

Seventeenth. At any annual meeting of the Board of Treasurers, or at any special meeting called for the purpose, the

Treasurers, representing a majority (in number and interest) of the members of the Association, may make such alterations in, and additions to, the aforegoing articles (excepting the eighth, fourteenth and fifteenth articles) as they may deem needful and proper.

Eighteenth. And whereas, the real estate, situate in said Lowell, formerly conveyed by the said Proprietors of the Locks and Canals on Merrimack River, to Luther Lawrence, Esq., since deceased, by deed dated August 1, 1838, recorded with Middlesex Deeds, Book 377, page 193, has been conveyed by his representatives to that corporation, by deed bearing even date herewith, upon the trusts and for the objects herewith, upon the trusts and for the objects herein before declared: Now the said Proprietors of the Locks and Canals on Merrimack River do hereby acknowledge and declare, that their free consent to become the grantees in said last mentioned deed was given at the execution, and delivery thereof, and that they stand possessed of and interested in the land and real estate, thereby conveyed to them, in trust, and for the uses, intents, and purposes, concerning the same herein expressed and contained,--and do hereby covenant with the several other corporations parties hereto, their associates, successors, and assigns, that the said Proprietors will hold and dispose of the said land and real estate upon and pursuant to the trusts, agreements, and provisions aforesaid.

IN WITNESS WHEREOF, the said Corporations, parties hereto, have caused this instrument to be sealed with their respective common seals, and to be signed by their respective officers, hereto duly authorized, the day and year first before written.

Signed, sealed, and delivered
in presence of us,

APPENDIX III

WHY DID THE LOWELL COTTON MILLS CLOSE?

By

JOHN ROGERS FLATHER
Member Lowell Historical Society

DELIVERED BEFORE
The Lowell Historical Society
Lowell, Massachusetts
April 20, 1972

Source: Center for Lowell History, Flather Collection

My fellow Members and Friends of the Lowell Historical Society:

About a year ago I think it was, Mr. Harry Dinmore spoke to me after church one Sunday and said that as they were going through the "old records" file of the Lowell Historical Society preparatory to moving to new quarters in the Lowell Technological Institute Library, he found many books and documents about the founding of Lowell and its extraordinary development throughout the 19th Century. However, he was astonished to find very little, if anything, about the decline and eventual closing of the Lowell mills. He thought I would be in a position to fill in this missing gap and asked if I'd consider preparing a paper to read.

As I was unable to do it at that time, it was scheduled for this Spring, so here we are.

It is distinctly my pleasure to be here this evening and to tell you some of the answers as I see them, and more particularly as I have lived through it all.

To understand the causes of the closing of the Lowell cotton mills and place things in perspective, may I first give a quick summary. Since my family was closely associated with the banking and business life in Lowell almost from its beginning, it might be well to commence this narrative with their involvement preceding me. My great grandfather James G. Carney and his bride Clarissa Willett came to Lowell on the Old Middlesex Canal on their honeymoon in 1828, and they liked it so much that we've been here ever since.

By way of documenting my earliest "credentials," the first slide is of the original letter written by Kirk Boott to Mr. Carney heartily supporting the discontinuance of the then existing policy of the Lowell mills in accepting deposits from the workers on interest, provided Mr. Carney should proceed with the establishment of the Lowell Institution for Savings in 1829, which Mr. Carney then proceeded to carry out.

Mr. Carney, Lowell

K. Boott – Jan. 17, 1829
Sav.s Inst. Pet

Dr. Sir –
I return you the petition
for a Savings institution –
If such an institution should be got up
& managed properly I have no doubt all
the companies here will discontinue to

190

receive money on interest - But for
one I have already so much business to attend
to that I should decline being connected with it –
though it has my hearty good wishes -
Yours truly
KIRK BOOTT

Jan. 17, 1829

I do not feel it necessary to go into the founding of the city which Harry has said is well recorded, except to say that the War of 1812 proved a catastrophe for the Boston importers whose incoming cargoes were seized by privateers. So, being innovators, they sought to manufacture cloth themselves. The Boston Manufacturing Company in Waltham proved the feasibility of making yarn and cloth here, and their only problem was that the Charles River provided very little water power. So they sent young Boott to Lowell and Mssrs. Appleton, Lowell, Jackson, and Lawrence, some of whom were Boott's relatives, provided the capital. The result was that Kirk Boott, with such strong financial backing and such dynamic ability on his own part, was able to not only succeed in establishing Lowell as the first Industrial City in the western hemisphere, but also in transferring the whole concept of the Industrial Revolution to the western hemisphere.

From this beginning, the spark was ignited which was to sweep America forward to its great industrial might, but the start had to be made somewhere and to this group of Boston merchants, Kirk Boott, and his associates goes the credit.

With this introduction, we now can trace through the events

and the causes leading up to the decline of the Lowell cotton mills.

It seems to me that the best way in which I can respond to the question before us is to draw upon my lifetime experience with one of the Lowell mills which I know most about, namely, the Boott Mills.

There is, of course, one objection in my doing so, that it will include my personal involvement. I can only hope that you will believe me when I say that this is not an attempt at any personal gain or credit on my part, or an attempt to prove that the action we took was correct, when as a matter of fact, we failed in the end to save the mill. But like the little boy who asked his father, "What did you do in the French Revolution, Daddy?", to which the father replied, "Well son, I survived." We survived.

Also, I have long desired to write up my life's work for my children and grandchildren which will account for some of the personal details which I will give you tonight.

I hasten to say that the views expressed here are largely my own, and I am sure there may have been some omissions which will no doubt come to me from thinking about this and talking with others for years to come.

Winston Churchill once said he could remember back several centuries because of events which were described and passed on to him from his parents, and to them from his grandparents and back through several previous generations.

The relevance of this is that continuity in a family enterprise (Lowell – Boott) furnishes succeeding generations with a knowledge of which the coming generations are heir. I can remember hearing my grandmother Rogers relate what her father James G. Carney told her, thus taking us back 140 odd years. One story will suffice: her father came back from the Lowell Institution for Savings one night and said that a depositor had accused him of giving the depositor three pennies too much change, and to which he proudly replied, "This bank never makes mistakes, and I never make mistakes, the three cents are yours."

My earliest recollections were of going to my grandfather Rogers' house after church on Sundays and wondering what the conversations meant when my grandfather said such things as "The Appleton Mills is going to have to be reorganized." Later, I overheard my grandfather tell my father as they were leaving the old Kirk St. Church, "I'm not walking home with you today, I have to go over and padlock the door of _____ Company because the Manager has been dishonest." At still another time, my Uncle John Jacob Rogers had just been elected to Congress (1912), and one of his early hopes was to introduce a bill in Congress to make the Merrimack River navigable so that Haverhill, Lawrence, and Lowell factories could receive cotton, coal, and other commodities at lower cost than overland. My grandfather died in 1914 and I was still in the Moody School, nearly a half century ago. As I grew older, I began to appreciate that I had been given an exposure to management problems in business at a very young age.

I recall the I.W.W. strike in 1912 when Joe Etta led a strike in Lawrence which spread up the river to Lowell, and clearly recall a group of workers marching up our hill asking where A.G. Cumnock's house was; he was Treasurer of the Appleton at the time.

These are just a few memories, but they sank in my mind, although I did not realize until many years later that there were labor problems to deal with, security, dishonesty, and watching over one's business, all very much a part of my preparation for life.

I could cite similar experiences from my grandfather Flather who came to this country from England in the middle 1850s at the age of about 16, started his own Flather Lathe Company in Nashua, NH, which burned down, following which my father had to go to work at the age of 12. I always remember his kindness in dealing with people and as one person said, "Joe always takes hold of the smooth handle."

My mother, grandmother, and grandfather Rogers, and my great grandmother and great grandfather Carney lived most of their adult life in Lowell. My father and my grandfather and grandmother Flather lived just across the Massachusetts line in Nashua.

With this background we are ready to list some of the causes for the closing of the Lowell mills and our attempted solutions to the problems besetting this area.

FIRST

I would like to confine my remarks from here on to the Boott Mills because that is what I know the most about. Comparisons will be made also to the problems affecting the six* large cotton weaving mills in Lowell, and also charts will be presented showing the problems of Massachusetts and New England in relation to Southern competition.

SECOND

As stated above, my thoughts will be based principally on my own experience and my various responsibilities in the management of the Boott Mills.

I entered the Boott Mills immediately after college and business school in 1923. My work was cut out for me. For two generations my family had been interested in the Boott Mills, which was founded in 1843. Earliest recollections of my family's lives were centered about "the mill." I was expected to enter it and always wanted to, and in the next quarter of a century I never deviated from trying to make the third generation as creditable as the preceding ones.

THIRD

I hope you will believe me when I express so many personal feelings in describing the nature and solutions of the problems that had to be solved.

FOURTH

I respectfully request permission to decline to answer any questions if in my personal judgment any comments would be indiscreet.

FIFTH

Since the mill closed in 1956, I have been working with Samson Cordage Works in the Executive Offices in Boston as Vice President in charge of purchasing for their mills in Shirley, MA, Icard, NC, Anniston, AL, and Vancouver, B.C. I have recently retired and have been serving as a Consultant, all of which is mentioned to explain why I do not feel it proper to give in this talk any information regarding Samson.

The next chart will show you that the handwriting was already on the wall that New England, Massachusetts, the Lowell Mills, and the Boott Mills were in trouble. (Charts of New England, Massachusetts, and Southern active spindles)

*I have omitted Lawrence Mfg. which was largely knitting.

I had been at the Boott Mills only 24 months when the Hamilton was in serious trouble in 1925 and had closed by 1927.

The Appleton was closed by 1929, the Tremont and Suffolk Mills by 1927, and the Massachusetts by 1929.

Only the Boott and the Merrimack remained, but they succeeded in lasting until 1956 in the case of Boott, and the early 1960s in the case of the Merrimack.

The closing of the Appleton, Hamilton, Tremont and Suffolk, and the Massachusetts Mills over a period of less than five years in a single community was nothing short of a tremendous upheaval in the Lowell economy and a catastrophe for the workers involved.

This was the result. Now we shall analyze the answer to the question at hand, "Why Did The Lowell Mills Close?"

The following reasons have been given:
. . . .

1. Southern competition
2. Labor unions
3. Higher cotton costs due to freight charges from the South to New England
4. Old machinery, old buildings, 5, 6, or 7-story buildings
5. Absentee management
6. Absentee ownership

7. Failure of the mills to put money into new machinery and to modernize

8. Practice of the mills to pay high dividends instead of putting money into modernization

9. Practice of the mills to continue making so called "grey" instead of selling finished cloth

10. Policy of the Massachusetts Legislature to pass social legislation which increased the cost of mills in Massachusetts compared with the South

11. Desirable as restrictive legislation was from a humane standpoint, it proved very inhumane when states and state legislatures literally next door to Massachusetts permitted 54 hours per week and/or even 60 hours per week in Maine, New Hampshire, Rhode Island and Connecticut, while Massachusetts was limited to 48 hours a week. Not until the New Deal came into effect in 1933 were more equal hours made mandatory.

12. As the situation of the Massachusetts mills worsened, the stockholders became more and more disenchanted with investments in cotton mills in Massachusetts.

13. City taxation, compared with a moratorium on taxes often offered by Southern communities to anyone who would build a mill in that community, placed Massachusetts and Lowell at a disadvantage.

14. The longer hours permitted in the South enabled mills to spread their overhead over a longer week and greater yardage. Also it enabled them to set up certain machinery and operate it on the same

construction of cloth without any down time for changeover to another construction. In contrast, the New England mills, and particularly the Lowell mills and the Boott Mills, were constantly changing to other products because of higher costs. The South had steady runs. Lowell and Boott had often only the "peak" runs.

15. Even though Lowell had its own water power, in many periods, dry summers and excessive freshet periods, steam power had to be resorted to. In the South, the advent of Duke and Alabama Power Company, etc. usually resulted in lower power costs than Lowell.

ANALYSIS OF THE ABOVE CAUSES WITH PARTICULAR REFERENCE TO ACTION TAKEN BY BOOTT MILLS, REFUSING TO THROW IN THE SPONGE:

It can be shown in detail that the Boott management had one idea and that was survival for the good of all concerned:

Southern competition was no myth. We have to start with the premise that the Southern mills enjoyed lower costs than Boott or other Lowell and New England mills. In the early part of the century, Southern mills did actually buy cotton from nearby plantations, but as cotton growing spread into Texas and Oklahoma this became less of a cost disadvantage to us, but damage was done while it lasted.

Power costs were lower and during the Depression, with the development of Duke and Alabama Power Company, lower power costs in the South resulted. True, Lowell had the advantage of its own water power as did other Massachusetts and New England mills. Although power is a small item, other cost advantages were available to the South from an excessive availability of labor, lower local taxes, more friendly legislation, longer hours permitted, and a more cooperative attitude on the part of Southern legislatures.

<u>LABOR UNIONS</u>

In my earlier days, the mill had local craft unions, such as "doffers" and "loom fixers," but beginning with the Depression and remedial federal legislation such as the National Recovery Act (NRA), national unions received a great boost and overall company unions also. A company-wide coverage by the CIO was supposed to benefit the workers both North and South, but for most of my experience the union had a difficult time organizing the South. This meant that the Southern mills enjoyed the advantage of being relatively new. Employers and people flocked to their mills without a thought of joining a union. As the people from New England farms found out when they came to Lowell, or people from Europe: "For the first time in their lives, these people had money in their pockets at the end of every two weeks." They were better off than they were on the farm, better off than when they were in Europe. Someone has said when an immigrant came to this country the first thing they needed was a job, and the cotton mill gave them that opportunity. But as time went on, people quite naturally became more choosy, welcomed help from the union, and the more the union became established in this area, the more anxious they were to improve working conditions. It was really a wonderful cycle of benefits which the Lowell mills provided. A regular job with regular pay has been described as the greatest Americanization factor available to people who came to our shores from foreign lands. A job in a cotton mill in New England became synonymous with a higher civilization and a better standard of living than on the farm or in the old country.

But all this time, the South was establishing itself in a stronger position because <u>their</u> people had not yet forgotten how much better off they were after the cotton mill moved into their valley, or how much worse off they were before the cotton mill came. This made it very difficult for the labor unions to get a stronghold in such Southern valleys.

As already mentioned, higher cotton costs generally did not prove insurmountable in the case of Boott trying to meet Southern competition. The real differentials were labor costs.

True, the mills did have old machinery in the North, old buildings, and multi-storied buildings. Boott was one of the first to put in "long-draft spinning" and "high speed looms."

ABSENTEE MANAGEMENT

Most of the top management of the Boott Mills, including myself, have lived in Lowell all our working lives. The Treasurer for many years was the Chief Executive Officer of the cotton mills in New England. Almost without exception, the Treasurer's Office of Lowell mills was in Boston where the financing was done in Boston banks and where the cotton brokers also had their offices. There were daily contacts in the Treasurer's Office in the case of Boott Mills where the Treasurer also bought the cotton. The President in the early part of this century was pretty apt to be less active in the operations of the mills, rarely visiting the mills, leaving that to a local "agent," and his principal function was being the Presiding Officer at Directors and Stockholders meetings. In the case of Boott, the Treasurer, my father, lived in Lowell as did I, and was within walking distance of the mill. My brother, Frederick, originally lived in Lowell, but left to live in Andover while continuing his work with Boott. In my case, I was always available for a hurried call to the mill and for no end of other local activities in carrying out the time-honored principle, "Watch your shop, or somebody else will." Father's regular schedule was to be at the mill in the early morning for an hour or so and then to take the 9:17 a.m. train to Boston. We always worked Saturday mornings, the entire office did, and often all day Saturday. In fact, I never knew what a five day week was until I had left Boott to work with Samson Cordage in Boston in 1956 to date.

FAILURE OF THE MILLS TO MODERNIZE

A simple reason for New England mills and more so in the case of Massachusetts, was the lack of incentive on the part of potential stockholders to invest their money in an area where they had to compete with lower cost mills in the South. Incentive was just not there, but Boott went against the trend in several particulars. As fast as Boott began to lose business to Southern mills quoting lower prices than Boott could quote, Boott took the initiative of integrating its processes, i.e. installed a bleachery, as finished goods commanded a relatively higher margin than the so-called gray (greige) goods. When this ran into lower cost bidding, we installed cutting and sewing machines and made a finished towel and finished curtain ready for consumer use and attractively packaged for retail selling.

The sewing was versatile, as we had both hemming and hem-stitching machines, automatic folding, automatic labeling, and automatic packaging.

TOWELS

After World War II, we made an intensive study of an automatic continuous sewing and assembly line production. I had the rare opportunity of going to New York and up to the Singer Tower to their so-called drafting and lay-out department where they designed for us a continuous towel line beginning at one end of a long mill room with a roll of cloth, cutting it into lengths, and feeding it onto a conveyor belt the length of No. 7 mill. Along the conveyor belt on each side were rows of the highest speed sewing machines Singer made at that time (Model #241), 5,000 stitches per minute. The stitching women were fed, via a conveyor belt, a neat pile of cut-to-length towels from the cutting machine. They were then sewed one towel at a time and the stitcher put the completed towel back on the same conveyor belt without having to move herself at all. The conveyor belt then brought the finished towels to the folding machine and then to the packaging.

At that time, Singer described it as the most modern towel sewing room in the entire industry. This was an example where Boott chose to spend its money for modernization in the finishing department, which eventually led into buying yarn and/or even cloth from the South at lower costs than could be spun and woven at Boott with a net saving which placed us nearer competition. Of course, the South again caught up with us, whereupon we would try to change to another product.

DEPRESSION

Since father took over the Boott Mills in 1905, we had changed from heavy cotton duck, heavy seamless grainbags, to toweling. Also, before the Depression and actually during World War I, father developed an excellent line of automobile tire fabric or tire duck, but that eventually all went to the South.

There were many other new products which time does not permit to describe in detail, but Boott had the best reputation for combed shoe duck which was so fine in texture one could write on it with a pencil. This had a good run for womens' shoes until it went out of vogue and we had to look for something else.

CORDOROY

Probably the most enterprising of all our efforts to survive was going into the finishing of corduroy: cutting the pile, brushing, and dyeing corduroy, a field which was limited to only four or five concerns in the United States. Boott at this time was actually making 25% of the gray corduroy (unfinished), but in the middle of the Depression the South began making gray corduroy at a much larger rate than previously, so we decided to go into finishing.

One of my duties was handling the selling with our sales agents in New York and Boston, and increasingly in New York. On one trip, our agents had an inquiry from a New York importer who was dealing with a concern in Holland, with the statement that they had tried out samples of corduroy from all the gray corduroy manufacturers who would send them and were convinced that Boott was making the best unfinished corduroy. The Dutch wanted their account to seriously consider doing some finishing in the U.S. and expressed a wish to discuss the possibility with Boott, so as to have the advantage of Boott quality.

The upshot of this was that in 1936 my wife and I went to Holland and spent several days at their plant. An amusing thing that happened was that the New York converter had cabled Holland that we were leaving on a certain date in August, but did not tell them when we were expected to arrive. As I was ushered into their office in Enschede, I was received by the son of the owner, when immediately thereafter the owner came in, speaking no English, but with a worried look which his son translated to mean that he didn't think I was the man they were expecting. We were there 1 ½ days earlier than he figured from the date of our sailing. I quickly explained to the son that we had sailed on the second voyage of the new Cunard Liner "Queen Mary," and that we had reached Southhampton, England in 4 ¾ days, or 1 ½ days earlier than he expected. The old gentleman could hardly believe it, not having any idea you could cross the Atlantic in that time.

The second day with the help of his interpreter, he told me his wonderful plan as follows:

"My factory is on the German border and Hitler is rattling the saber. I have seen the German Army in my factory twice within my life time (1870 and 1914). It is going to happen a third time, and I have decided to hedge by sending a third of my finishing machinery, a third of my wealth, and one of my three sons to America."

It was a once in a lifetime experience, and after I returned I talked it over with my associates in Lowell and we invited the son to visit us, which took more time, but eventually he came. By then it was 1937 and Hitler was on the verge of or perhaps had already moved into the Sudetenland. However, the son did come to Boston and we spent half a night talking to him. He was tremendously enthusiastic and so were we. He returned to Holland, we had a fine letter from him, but by then and before plans could be put into effect, it was too late. Labor Day, 1939, World War II began.

NAVY TWILL

Of course, the United States was not in the war until December 7, 1941, but Boott was in real trouble meeting competition in toweling and gray corduroy, so a trip to New York unearthed a small trial order from the Navy for uniform twill. For many months, this opened up a most fortuitous development which never ended until World War II ended. We not only qualified as meeting all the Navy specifications, but their reliance on us grew rapidly so that by the time the United States entered the war we had become the Navy's largest supplier of white uniform twill. This involved many rearrangements at the mill which were necessary to meet ever-expanding production from a normal work force of 1500 employees. By 1942, 1943 and 1944, we were required to maintain a force of close to 2500 employees, and in one year we processed 5000 employees to try to maintain the 2500 total. I served on the local appeal board, the local War Production Board. We were always in trouble because we had no cost-plus contracts, and we were entirely at the mercy of Southern competitors, of which there were 6 to 8 bidders on every Navy offering. The Navy issued no cost-plus contracts to the textile industry and as far as a mill in Lowell was concerned, we had to compete for workers with Remington Arms, South Lowell (before Raytheon moved in). Also our skilled help were leaving us, commuting to Charlestown Navy Yard and Fore River Shipyard, and some of them were even buying mobile homes and living in the South Portland shipyard area, Bath, and many went to Portsmouth Navy Yard. So we were always in difficulty in holding help and in desperation I went to the Department of Education of the State of Massachusetts and told them we wanted to train supervisors, to not only train fixers, but also to train our supervisors in personnel relations. By this we meant treating people fairly and in a friendly way so that we could hold onto them and so that they would be happy to stay with us once we had trained them.

At the same time, we arranged with the Lowell Trade School to give us a room and with the help of the State Department of Education who supplied us with a teacher, he and I conducted a course one night a week for several months. At the end of that course we were asked by the Navy to write up a manual for training employees and/or supervisors which was subsequently put out and circulated throughout the textile industry all over the United States.

This enabled us to offset to an extent the piracy by nearby concerns for our skilled employees who had the advantage of cost-plus prices.

ARMY-NAVY-E

At the dedication and award celebration, the Navy was well represented and all our staff and employees took part. We were heralded as the first cotton mill in New England to receive the Army Navy E pennant, and at the end of the war we were the only cotton mill in the United States to have received four stars on our pennant. The government had three criteria for winning these awards.

1. That we had volunteered to do Navy work prior to Pearl Harbor (we were at least two years before Pearl Harbor)
2. That close to 100% of our production was on government work
3. That we had done something outstanding and unique on our own for the war effort, and in this we qualified by our training school and the fact that the War Production Board distributed our manual throughout the country

This was a big day for the mill and a big day for Lowell. There was only one bitter angle to all of this war performance and that was the cutbacks after the Armistice in 1945 which crippled us. But we faced up to the problem of the long, hard struggle to get back on our civilian and peace-time products. This we did, but at a considerable cost with the result that profits were low and at times we incurred losses.

Also as will be shown in Chart No. 20, the North-South wage differential had widened, while during the war it had narrowed.

DECLINE IN NEW ENGLAND, MASSACHUSETTS, AND LOWELL IN ACTIVE COTTON SPINDLES

The active cotton spindles in the South increased steadily from 1906 to 1930. In the Depression and from then on they remained at the same level in comparison with Massachusetts, in which the active cotton spindles remained more or less static throughout World War I. They began to tumble sharply beginning in 1923, ironically in the very year I started at the Boott Mills. The Massachusetts spindles plunged from 11 million active spindles in 1923 to 1 million approximately in 1956, compared with 17 million in the South.

CITY TAX APPEAL

We sought relief from the city for a reduction in local taxes which was denied and which forced us to avail ourselves of appealing before the Board of the Massachusetts Tax Abatements Division, which we won.

THE UNION IN POST WAR PERIOD

We also sought the help of our labor union (CIO) with whom we discussed our overall problem. In fairness to them, the union had I think only one mill unionized in this area, Boott. This union had been more or less accepted by us during the war boom at the request of the Navy who warned us over and over again not to have a strike during the war. We of course complied with this and there was no strike during the war. But from 1946 to 1950, we were in a squeeze even though I made personal trips to the union office and attended a long meeting to try to work out a wage reduction with tentative approval from the committee and the Business Agent, all of whom promised they would vote to approve the plan the next day. However, I was told that the vote was unanimously "no." We had reasonably pleasant discussions, but they were in a bind also trying to keep the only mill they had on their books, so to speak, and that was the Boott Mills. We finally reached an impasse in 1947, October, and a strike occurred which lasted for eight months until April, 1948. This was not an angry strike at anytime, but it was a costly one. The community as a whole took no sides, the press understood the problems, and we never asked the police to do anything more than keep things calm so that those who wished to work could work. This was largely limited to supervisory employees who made it possible to keep our products alive in the markets in which we sold. In retrospect, in all sincerity, the strike was necessary. It solved the problems of each of us, of the mill and the union, but it was a mistake and a tragedy for both sides.

If any of you watched the Queen Elizabeth picture on Channel 2 in March, you may remember that at the time when the Spanish, the English, and the French were jockeying for control of the seas, and hence control of their economic position, she said in great seriousness, "It's a hard bargain when both parties are losers."

Critics of the New England mills often say that they ought to have moved South rather than having to close eventually in New England. Speaking principally for the Boott Mills and the stockholders of the Boott Mills, the charts showing the steady increase in Southern spindle and the plunge in the Massachusetts curve would make any stockholder wary of investing any money in a Northern textile mill. In the 1950s when the Boott closed, it was because it was no longer feasible to continue it even though as the new buyer said, "We like the Boott product, we like the reputation they have throughout the country, we like their policy of equipping themselves to make finished, ready to use cloth, even though the mill buildings themselves are old."

Finally, it is unavoidable evidence that three of the Lowell mills which did have Southern mills for many years closed. (Appleton, Merrimack, and Pepperell had bought the Massachusetts mills in Lowell, and Pepperell already had a Southern mill.) The Southern mills did not save the Lowell mills.

Appendix IV

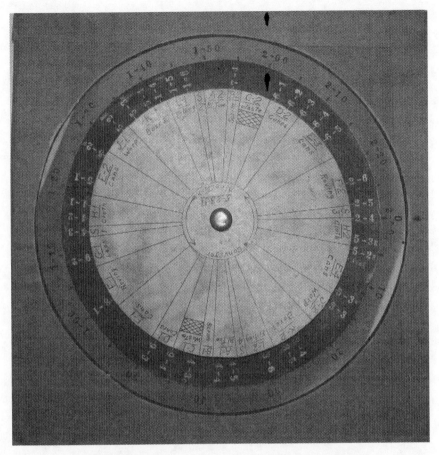

Conveyor System Guide for Employees (1951)

Afterward

Rog died on November 22, 2004. He completed the manuscript for this book while ill with cancer. I am pleased that it is finally being published.

I would like to thank my daughter Lisa Flather, the book's editor.

I would like to thank my nephew John Haddad for his contribution to the early editing process.

I would like to thank my brother-in-law, Newell Flather for his help with the book's cover photograph and for his careful review of the final draft.

I would like to thank Jack Herlihy of the Lowell National Historic Park and Martha Mayo of the Center of the Lowell History for attending to our every request.

Finally, I would like to thank the staff at Author House for their patient advice and assistance in the completion of this project.

Rebecca Flather

New York, New York
August, 2010